Hashtags and Revolutions: Unra
Spring and Hong Kong's Umbrel

Table of Contents

Abstract

Hashtags and Revolutions: Unraveling Arab Spring and Hong Kong's Umbrella Movement" offers a captivating and in-depth analysis of the pivotal role played by social media in two groundbreaking social and political movements. This unique book takes readers on a compelling journey through the modern history of digital activism, exploring how online platforms became powerful tools for change during the Arab Spring and the Hong Kong Umbrella Movement.

In these pages, readers will gain a profound understanding of how social media platforms, such as Twitter, Facebook, and Instagram, facilitated the mobilization, organization, and dissemination of information during these movements. The book explores how hashtags and viral content empowered individuals to unite, express dissent, and challenge established authorities.

Through meticulous research and firsthand accounts, "Hashtags and Revolutions" unveils the intricate dynamics of these movements, shedding light on the strategies employed by activists and the responses of governments and authorities. It also delves into the impact of these movements on both local and global politics, as well as their lasting influence on the world of digital activism.

Introduction

When I wait for the bus or have lunch alone, I habitually check my friends' statuses and comments on social media. When social media did not exist and mobile phones were not all that smart, reading a book was my favourite activity. Literary stories were attractive and addictive, and I could feel an emotional connection to the characters in my imaginary world. When I pictured the narratives in my mind, my experiences and knowledge of the actual world served as the foundation. My mood fluctuated with the narratives and my actual world was gradually extended through my immersion in the imaginary realm.

Even though I no longer carry a book with me, social media gives me a similar experience of an extended reality. While the medium has changed from a book to a selection of networked applications, and literary narratives have been replaced by the stories of my friends, formed by texts, emojis, pictures, videos, and memes, the feeling of extension remains the same. Now, I feel that another domain exists online, which is other than the world that I physically live in. This is an extension of the actual world that I would like to call the 'virtual world'. Unlike the imaginary world I connect to while reading a book, the virtual world is no longer bound to my own mind, but open to anyone who uses social media. The virtual world expands through instant global connections, thrives on content generation and sharing, and facilitates communication in interpersonal networks. My reality, in fact, is composed of both the actual and the virtual worlds.

Here, I embrace Marshal McLuhan's idea regarding our new and extended reality in the virtual world, put forward in his remarkable work *Understanding Media: The Extension of Man* (1964). McLuhan asserts that the extension of man results from "the new scale that is introduced into our affairs" (1964, p. 7) by new technological media. In other words, people's abilities are developed and their sensorium is extended by using the new media. The message of the medium is the role it plays in society, as well as the further capabilities it affords to humans, rather than the literal messages it contains. Developing on McLuhan' idea, I approach social media as a gateway that offers its users 'an extension of man' into the virtual world, where human sensoria and people's capacity to interact with others are transformed. This transformation is especially notable in contemporary social movements. Social media enables activists to mediate[1] their emotions and record protests for their audiences, while direct interaction through social media also allows them to share and explain their political stance, in order to provoke potential activists to act (Lee et al. 2017). In particular, this thesis regards both activists and audiences as social media users. Activists actively participate in social movements, while audiences are usually onlookers to the action. However, audiences may potentially become activists

---

[1] The idea of mediation has been used to describe how media represents external reality to human beings (Bolter & Grusin 2000). For example, when readers approach the world through a novel, the world is being mediated by the texts in that book. Similarly, with social media use, the actual world is mediated through content shared in social networks.

themselves through social media interaction.

Here, it is necessary to address what social movements mean in this thesis. Although there is no universally agreed definition for social movements, according to Roggeband and Klandermans (2010), it be concluded that social movements take place when people gathering to form various collective actions (including riots, demonstrations, sit-ins, strikes and so on) driven by diverse and multifaceted forms of mobilisation in order to achieve or resist social or political changes. To expand, social movements can be understood through different perspectives; for instance, through a structural approach (e.g. unequal distribution of resources and rights), a cultural approach (e.g. interpretation of words, arts, events and so on), and social psychology (e.g. collective identity and emotions) (Jasper 2010; Smith & Fetner 2010; van Stekelenburg & Klandermans 2010). This thesis believes that social media use in thecurrent decade has created new conditions for the approaches above and developed social movements into a new form.

Furthermore, social media has the capacity to extend local issues into global phenomena. Evidence of this can be observed from, for instance, the Occupy Wall Street movement (OWS) and the Arab Spring in 2011, the Berish ('Clean' in

Malaysian) rallies in 2013, and the Hong Kong Umbrella Movement in 2014.[2]

Through international communications and the diffusion of information on social

media, the influence of social movements is augmented (Kim et al. 2014). More local

residents and those spread to other regions through diaspora are summoned to the

movements and the global atmosphere of social movements becomes inflamed (Chen

et al. 2015; Jurgenson 2012). Furthermore, through the use of social media, a

'rhizomatic assemblage'[3] gradually replaces the hierarchical formation of the social

movements and becomes the major force leading protests (Lim 2017).

Many scholars argue that while it is apparent that social media use in contemporary

social movements is increasing, it is not valid to call those movements "social media

revolutions", since social media is a platform for communication rather than a cause

of uprisings (Gladwell 2010; Huat 2017; Hands 2011; Jurgenson 2012; Lee 2015b;

Morozov 2011a). This thesis also endorses this idea, but further concentrates on the

relationship between social media and its users and how it enhances the users'

capabilities in relation to the dynamics of organisation, mobilisation, and contagion in

---

[2] According to Lim (2017), Lee et al. (2016), Rane and Salem (2012) and Skinner (2011), the Occupy movement spread across the US and the UK; the Arab Spring involved most Middle Eastern countries; the Berish rallies were supported by a large amount of local residents and Malaysians living abroad; and the Umbrella Movement summoned both local citizens and oversea "Hongkongers" to act together.

[3] Lim (2017) uses this term to describe a group of people connected by the horizontal friend-to-friend network on different social media platforms. Developing upon Deleuze and Guattari's (2004) idea, Lim regards the network as a particular "line of f(l)ight", a horizontal alliance where the multiplicities in a network can interact with each other.

and between the current social movements. Against this background, the thesis asks: what is the role of social media in contemporary social movements?

In order to answer this question, I will elaborate on how social media changes the environment of communication in social movements, how activists operate in social movements through social media, and how social movements travel from one region to the next through social media. In answering these questions, I intend to rework the idea of how social media has been used in social movements such as the Arab Spring and the Hong Kong Umbrella Movement. This thesis will perceive social media as a 'bridge', linking and communicating with both actual and virtual dimensions of reality. Through social media use, the virtual dimension overlays on the actual world and the concept of time and space has been reset (Potts 2015). At the same time, it is worth considering that social media is becoming essential to the activists in current movements as a 'natural' extension of themselves and their physical function – even before it becomes a weapon for them in to use in the fight against their opponents, they use it to talk (mouth), to listen (ears), to see (eyes), to experience a wider range of feeling (heart), and to record (memory).[4]

This thesis targets a gap in previous scholarship concerning the relationship between social media and social movements. On one hand, it has been customary to regard

---

[4] This connects McLuhan's idea of 'extension' with the post-humanist notion of 'cyborg' (e.g. Haraway 2013) to view social media as a necessary component, or a new "organ", of the human body.

social media merely as a technology based tool that relates to interpersonal

communication in the virtual world, but has no relation to social movements in the

actual world (see e.g. see Gladwell 2010 and Morozov 2011a); on the other hand,

there is a belief that a virtual world of peace, justice, and freedom has been

constructed in social media, where issues haunting the actual world can be 'virtually'

solved (see e.g. Shirky 2008). These studies perceive the actual and virtual worlds as

independent and exclusive domains and ignore the potential for interaction between

them. Therefore, what is missing is an integrated approach that considers social media

as a bridge between the two worlds and rethinks its effect on current social

movements.

Additionally, my research reveals the connection between different social movements

in terms of the similarity of patterns in large protests, which is rarely discussed in

existing research.[5] As social media is frequently involved with the social movements

in this present era, this thesis argues that not only that the diffusion of activism is

possible, but that using social media to unite activists and augment protest is

becoming a common trend. This trend will further affect and enlighten movements in

other regions. This research does not discuss the causes and effects of social

movements, or discuss their valence in the fields of politics or international relations.

Rather, the focus is on the active role of social media and its incorporation by activists

---

[5] Recently, the underlying connections in East Asian social movements in the past decade has been implied in Huat (2017).

into social movements.

In this project, I follow the idea that as well as the 'actual world' in which humans physically occupy, there is a 'virtual world' overlapping it. The virtual world is constructed on the basis of Information Communication Technologies (ICTs) and with clusters of data and programs. Together, both worlds together build up an "augmented reality" (Jurgenson 2012).[6] To expand on this idea, I assume that through social media, activists are able to immerse themselves simultaneously in the actual and the virtual worlds. Even though they are not directly linked to each other in the actual world, they are still 'close' online.

So, what does 'augmented reality' mean to contemporary social movements? First, Social media enables activists to construct their own 'stories' online. Notably, this thesis distinguishes these stories from news stories published through mass media that

---

[6] Nathan Jurgenson (2012) describes the actual world as the domain which is composed of "atoms" and regards the virtual world as another realm constructed with algorithms of 1 and 0, or "bits" in computer science. He argues that the digital and physical enmesh to form an "augmented reality", where social media links the power of the digital with the power of the physical, offering current revolutions a new form.

promote government policies (Herman & Chomsky 2002).[7] The stories 'published' on social media reflect issues in the actual world through texts, pictures, audio, and video from the activists' perspectives. At the same time, these stories consist of the activists' experiences and emotional factors. While social media extends the users' sensations to the virtual world, the audiences who read those stories – like reading a book – may have aroused in them a similar emotion, and then resonate with the activists at a distance. Even though the audiences do not physically participate in a movement, they can engage digitally through the social media content. Gradually, audiences may become potential activists. Thus, when a movement in the actual world is diffused digitally, it enters the virtual world where global connections take place and public opinion is reshaped, it can draw attention to its operations and summon supporters on a global scale.

We may mistakenly believe that audiences will gain a full understanding of the actual circumstances of social movements through exposure to social media content. In fact, similarly to mass media, what the audiences learn from social media and engage with

---

[7] Edward Herman and Noam Chomsky (2002) highlight that the news releases from mass media are prone to government interference and thus mostly favour the political opinion of the government. They note five filters applied to news writing and publishing in this model. They are (1) Ownership: the political position of the media owner will affect the opinions of the news; (2) Advertising: the media always favour their sponsors for economic interests; (3) Sourcing: the supply of news materials is controlled by big news agencies; (4) Flak: the fear of negative response to the news reports; and (5) Fear: the news intends to create an "enemy" and pose it as a potential threat (which either real, exaggerated or imaged) to the public in order to generate negative discourse against the "enemy" and simultaneously transfer the public focus from domestic political issues to outside ones.

has been 'framed'[8] and limited by the fragments filtered by the activists (Goffman

1974; Pan & Kosicki 1993). Furthermore, social media, which functions with

algorithms of 'big data', aims to provide user-preferred content for its users,

according to their search history (van Dijck 2013). In other words, even if the virtual

world is conceived as an extension of the actual world, audiences can hardly

understand the full picture of an actual remote event via social media. On the other

hand, knowing a social movement through mass media may be restricted by the

governing power; social media, thus, gradually becomes the source of information for

the users and international mainstream media.

Additionally, the audiences' consumption of the stories shared in the virtual world

will result in changes in their understanding or their need to take action in the actual

realm. According to previous studies, virtual communication between activists,

combined with physical occupation, is a crucial feature in current social movements

(see e.g. Lee 2017; Lee et al. 2017; Lim 2017; Wang 2017a). This can be seen as an

outcome of the integration of the virtual world on the actual world. It is important,

then, to understand how issues in the digital domain affect the protest actions in the

physical domain via social media, or how activists motivate audiences through their

---

[8] Pan and Kosicki (1993) acknowledge that news media plays an active role to construct discourse of public policy issues. They conceive the news as a frame of an issue from the journalist's perspective. Framing explains how the journalist organises his sources to guide the audiences to a specific discourse. Here, even though the posts of the activists are not 'news' in the conventional sense, they work as news feed on social media. Also, I regard activists equipped with social media as journalists of a knid. In other words, the activists actually frame the movements through social media and their framings will guide the discourse among their audiences.

posts. I believe that mobilisation relates not only to the activists' rhetoric – which

reforms the audiences' impression of the movement, arouses emotions, and motivates

them to act – but is also relates to the interpersonal relations on social media (Agarwal

et al. 2014; van Dijck 2013; Rheingold 2002).

Furthermore, this thesis will point out that social media, in fact, can inflame the

atmosphere of social movements to a global level; local audiences can be affected by

social movements in other regions, and vice versa. As a social movement extends to

both the actual and virtual worlds, it becomes what Jurgenson (2012) calls: an

'augmented revolution'. Here, public opinion is shaped via interactions in the virtual

world; activists operate in physical and digital spaces and communities take form

online and offline. By establishing the model of augmented revolutions, this thesis

points out new directions of structure, organisation, mobilisation, and contagion for

understanding social movements in the era of social media.

This thesis conducts a comparative analysis of two remarkable social movements, the

Arab Spring and the Hong Kong Umbrella Movement, to investigate the role of social

media in generating 'augmented revolution'. These cases are *atypical* in comparison

to traditional social movements where participants rely less on digital

communications and more on actual, physical actions on the street. However, these

two movements are also *typical* augmented revolutions because both featured the

intense involvement of social media in terms of organisation, recording, dissemination, and mobilisation. This case study also recognises that the movements were completely different in terms of goals, cultural background, ICTs infrastructure, and political and economic developments. At the same time, the movements did not remain limited to their local regions, but quickly resonated with audiences on social media around the world and became global events with online and offline participation. By studying and comparing these two movements, this thesis not only intends to demonstrate how the movements worked under the model of augmented revolution, but also wants to prove that contemporary social movements can travel from one region to another regardless of the context with the facility of social media.

In order to investigate the activists' operations and intentions and how audiences were influenced through social media, this study focuses on the social media content shared during the movements. It is believed that in augmented revolution, the interactions between activists and audiences are mainly based on posting and sharing on social media. Thus, social media content is the key to generate impact on audiences, and at the same time, to reveal activists' intentions. To this end, this thesis will adopt textual analysis (McKee 2003) to interpret the social media materials shared during the Arab Spring and Hong Kong Umbrella Movement. According to McKee (2003), textual analysis is a qualitative method for interpreting texts (including films, pictures, television programmes, clothes and so on) in order to obtain a sense of the ways in which, in particular cultures at particular times, people make sense of the world around them. By applying textual analysis, the impact of social media use on the cultural and psychological approaches to contemporary social movements will be

discovered.

Additionally, activists used framing in constructing their posts as they 'virtualise' the

movements – they worked as citizen journalists with social media. Thus, 'framing

analysis'[9] (Pan & Kosicki 1993) is applied in this study in order to analyse the textual

materials shared on Facebook. Indeed, framing analysis explains how journalists

(here, activists) use framing devices (metaphors, exemplars, catchphrases, depictions

and visual images) to package and deliver information to their audiences (Gitlin 1980;

Gamson & Modigliani 1989). At the same time, it demonstrates how the content can

be interpreted differently, how interpretations are location-specific and how they

evoke different emotions (Goffman 1974; Boulding 1959). By adopting this method, I

aim to discover the hidden meanings and the influences of selected posts, and the

purposes behind influential Facebook groups and protesters. In particular, Facebook

posts that were shared during the movements by influential accounts which were

recognised as 'leaders' and posts that demonstrated the situations on protest sites will

---

[9] Pan and Kosicki (1993) lists four structures of the news article to be focused in the framing analysis. They are syntactical, script, thematic and rhetorical structure. Basically, the syntactical structure relates to the traditional "inverted pyramid" in news writing, where the more valuable information would be mentioned in front. However, it could be organised into various orders according to different purposes. Also, quotation of the empirical evidence and official sources plays an important role in articles. Thus, this structure can indicate how the activists value the facts within one issue and use evidence to persuade readers. Analysing the script structure helps researchers to discover how the writers use the elements, 5W (who, when where, what, why) and 1H (how), to organise their viewpoints and show their concentration. On the other hand, thematic structure relates the logical hypothesis that the articles (here, posts) potentially propose, or predict in order to guide audiences' thinking, when several related issues are mentioned at once. Finally, the rhetorical structure focuses on the style of writing.

be studied in this thesis. By studying these posts, this thesis intends to find out how the actual world was virtualised and, in turn, how the posts influenced the actions in the actual world.

Finally, this thesis argues that although social media plays an important role in contemporary social movements, it is still a product of capitalism and is controlled by giant transnational corporations. Social media like Facebook and Twitter have their own limitations: they have a primary mission to accomplish, which is to maximise the profit of their owners, and when given access to a new regional market they need to obey the rules and policies of local governance and respect the local culture. Also, social media must keep evolving in order to survive in global competition, with new functions constantly being added, bringing a degree of uncertainty to its future operations in social movements.

This thesis contains five sections. It starts with a Literature Review, which considers how social media changes the environment for public participation in social movements and reforms the global communication conditions for the emergence of augmented revolutions. Then, Chapter 1 provides an introduction to the Arab Spring and the Umbrella Movement in the era of social media. Chapter 2 and 3 both discuss the activists' social media operations during the protests and the ways in which social movements become augmented and international. In particular, Chapter 2 focuses on how the actual world is virtualised via social media, while Chapter 3 concentrates on how the virtual activities and interactions are actualised and impact the actual world

with social media use. Conclusions and propositions for future research will be made

at the end.

Literature Review

This literature review will cover relevant existing scholarship in order to understand how social media changes the environment of communication in social movements; how activists operate in social movements through social media; and how social movements travel from one region to the next through social media. By articulating the relationship among activists, social media, and social movements, this literature review maps answers to these questions and fosters an in-depth understanding of the role of social media in social movements.

The global digital sphere for social movements

We may recognise the significant changes in our daily working and social lives in recent decades: emails have become a necessary part of work related communication; searching engines, such as Google, have become primary sources of knowledge; 'live streams' are no longer limited to television, but can be easily found on YouTube, or Twitch; making friends, regardless of their background or distance, is just one click away – 'Add Friend' on Facebook or 'Follow' on Twitter; mobile phones have become smarter; and all of these 'apps' can be accessed at any time through a slight movement of a thumb or finger. It is not difficult to observe that with the ongoing development of Information Communication Technologies (ICTs), interpersonal communication is being digitalised and extended to a global scale (Hands 2011;

Rantanen 2005; Tehranian 1999; Thussu 2000). Social network sites (SNSs), known

as online platforms (such as Facebook, Twitter, LinkedIn) dramatically enhance

international communication and reform the social lives of their users (van Dijck

2013).[10] Through the use of those social media, "the world grows increasingly

virtual" (Jurgenson 2012, p. 86).

In this present era, an open digital domain for global communication is emerging. In

this thesis, I call it the "global digital sphere", since its main features are the

globalisation and digitalisation of communication. The concept of the global digital

sphere is crucial to understanding 'augmented revolution'. As Jurgenson (2012)

demonstrates, social media offers a promise to activists: when they shout through

Facebook or Twitter, they shout into a network made up of bits, "a network where

there may be an audience receptive to the message" (p. 88). Messages shared by

activists through social media may finally reach anyone, anywhere, due to global

---

[10] Van Dijck (2013) distinguishes various types of social media and allocates them into four big categories: (1) "social network sites (SNSs)" that aim to promote interpersonal contact, such as Facebook, Twitter, LinkedIn, Google+; (2) "user-generated content (UGC)" through sites that support creativity, promote and share professional content, such as YouTube, Wikipedia; (3) "trading and marketing sites (TMSs)", such as Amazon and eBay; and (4) "play and game sites (PGS)" that gathers players of popular games to share and discuss their experience of the games. This thesis focuses on the SNSs.

connections in the virtual world.[11] This promise implies an outcome of the emergence

of the global digital sphere which is important for this thesis: the global spread of

social movements.

Social media and the emergence of the global digital sphere

Social media users seem to hold a fond hope for the virtual world, in which they enjoy

not only global connection, but also 'freedom of speech'. I believe that social media

use has partly realised expectations in connection with the development of ICTs, and

that a freely and globally connected world has been established. Some scholars, also,

speak of the free flow of information on social media (Ayish 2001; van Aelst &

Walgrave 2004; van de Donk et al. 2004; Madikiza & Bornman 2007). This idea has

developed from the argument that media should expose public issues on a large scale,

foster wider public participation in the political process and, simultaneously, facilitate

public supervision of the behaviour of the government (Madikiza & Bornman 2007).

From this perspective, I review the role of social media in the current decade. The

capacity and use of social media – to compose, to share, to network, all without

---

[11] Some scholars, such as Wong et al. (2009) and Wijetunge (2014), argue that the world is still not globally connected due to the existence of a "digital divide". Some regions do not have access to the Internet because of low economic development and the lack of ICT infrastructures. I agree with this viewpoint. However, as this thesis focuses on the role of social media in current social movements, the digital divide is not a major concern. On the other hand, attention and interest gaps which indicate that people may have no time or interest for political discussions should be consider in the future. This thesis assumes that social media users have enough time to explore social media contents and are willing to participate in political discussions.

interference – indeed reflects the idea of freedom of expression and realises what is

referred to by Shirky (2011) as "Internet freedom".[12] Social media becomes an

alternative news source, since it can circumvent the interference of governments and

corporations on traditional news production (Boykoff 2006; Herman & Chomsky

2002). Social media enables direct and instant digital communication, enhancing the

freedom of the public to participate in public issues. According to Shirky (2008;

2011), social media is a "long-term tool" that can strengthen civil society and the

public sphere through fostering public participation and communicative freedom.[13]

Thus, the free flow of information through ICTs is already embedded in the role of

social media – the prevalent use of social media has laid the foundation for freedom

of participation and expression in the digital sphere.

On the other hand, social media amplifies the trend of globalisation in the digital

sphere (Rantanen 2005; Tehranian 1999; Thussu 2000), an idea that can be traced

back to McLuhan's statement about the "global village"[14] (1964). According to

Robertson (1992), globalisation is the representation of the awareness that people

---

[12] Shirky (2011) regards Internet freedom as the freedom to access information, the freedom of ordinary citizens to produce their own public media and the freedom of citizens to converse with one another.

[13] Shirky (2008; 2011) also argues that many people only regard social media as a short-term coordinating tool for all of the world's political movements, but social media, indeed, has the ability to change the society on the long run.

[14] McLuhan (1964) uses this metaphor to envisage that the world, or the globe, shirks into a "village" through electronic technology and the information can move instantly and freely from one point to another.

have of the world as a whole. It can also refer to the fact that local events can be influenced by events in distant locations, and vice versa (Giddens 1990).

Globalisation combined with the free flow of information on social media, make possible a borderless community and worldwide cooperation in addressing global issues (Bauman 1998; Bornman & Schoonraad 2001; Rantanen 2005; Thussu 2000; Waters 1995). Additionally, as people in any locality can experience global events by connecting on social media, they are actually exposed to the influence of the knowledge, values, and behaviours formed in other regions and cultures[15] (Giddens 1991). Globalisation theory would seem to imply the possibility of global diffusion of social movements through social media.

In sum, the free flow of information over the Internet is a demonstration of how information is disseminated in the virtual world; and globalisation theory illustrates how the information shared in the virtual world through social media may impact on the actual world. The result of these process is the global digital sphere. By using social media, activists' messages can move freely and globally in the digital sphere and then affect potential activists in remote regions. I believe that the global digital sphere will provide a better understanding of the inflammable atmosphere of social

---

[15] This idea can also be understood from the perspectives of the Social Learning Effects (Bandura 1986; 2002) and the Socialisation Effects (McQuail 2005). The former suggests that individuals cannot learn everything from direct personal experience. In this case, media becomes an additional source of knowledge. The latter further stresses that audiences can learn how to behave in a specific situation through media representations. These ideas demonstrate the audiences' learning processes and indicate the power of media content and the necessity to understand what has been mediated, or framed, in the content.

movements today.

However, the global digital sphere is facing certain challenges: one is the argument

that its information flow is not truly free and is, rather, restricted by many factors,

such as language, software, and economic and political power (Madikiza & Bornman

2007); and it has been argued that excessive freedom is harmful to social stability

(Ayish 2001).The trend of globalisation in the digital sphere has also been involved

with the debate concerning cultural imperialism and cultural convergence and

divergence (Ayish 2005; Galtung 1971; Thussu 2000).[16] These criticisms are

important to bear in mind when applying the concept of global digital sphere to an

inquiry into social media.

The global digital sphere and the digital public sphere

Public opinion is the key to gathering protesters to take part in contemporary social

movements (Shirky 2011). Additionally, Jurgen Habermas (1989) proposes the idea of

the "public sphere", to aid understanding of public political communication and the

construction of public opinion. In this thesis, I borrow Habermas' idea to view the

---

[16] Cultural imperialism has been discussed in dependency theory and structural theory of
imperialism (Ayish 2005; Galtung 1971). They highlight the imbalance of information flow
between the developed and developing countries. Cultural imperialism also leads to the debate
about cultural convergence and divergence. Cultural convergence means that the culture in the
developing countries aligns with what of the developed countries, which has also been referred to
as Westernisation or Modernisation. Cultural divergence suggests that the diversity of culture
should be preserved from cultural imperialism (Thussu 2000).

global digital sphere as becoming the digital public sphere in the era of social media.

Habermas' public sphere is an open and unrestricted arena where a group of individuals can participate in a rational-critical debate on political issues, social norms, and ideas (Duvenhage 2005; Thussu 2000).[17] The rationality of the public sphere can extend to embrace other classes and groups (Habermas 1987; 1989; 1992). Public opinion, formed as a result of debate in the public sphere, stands up for the general interest and challenges the general governing relations (Habermas 1989). However, Habermas (1989) also recognises that private property (information as a commodity under capitalism) and personal skills (access to education) are required in order to participate in the public sphere. Other scholars further argue that the public sphere, in fact, favours the interests of only the classes that have power in terms of politics, economics, and culture and excludes marginalised groups such as the poor, women, and racial minorities (Fraser 1992; MacKee 2005; Negt & Kluge 1993; Pateman 1989; van Zoonen 2005).[18] Habermas (2006) added that the development of the consumer culture and the growing power of interest groups in mass

---

[17] Habermas firstly investigates the bourgeois public sphere in 18th century salons. He finds that private people come together as a public, the public sphere developing from the intimate family. It is a place where the public can have critical reflections on political issues based on individuals' private experience; the public authority, with control over the public sphere, was contested and "wrested away by the critical reasoning of private person on political issues" (Habermas 1989, p. 29-30).

[18] The scholars here, in other words, believe that the public sphere is dominated by the powerful groups which occupy the political system, own resources and the lobbying power, control the media system and address the public opinion with agenda setting and framing. The public sphere, finally, would convert into another place of promoting government policies and merchandise.

communication in the modern age have changed the status of the public sphere and the formation of public opinion. According to Habermas (1989; 2001; 2006), as the public has become culture-consuming rather than debating, the principle of rational-critical political debate to construct public opinion has been lost.

So, how does the public sphere change in this present era? First, with the social media use, the debate on public issues can now take place in the virtual dimension (Lee et al. 2015). Second, since the global digital sphere is free to access, marginalised groups that have been excluded in the actual world can now join the discussion, easily and equally, through social media (Asen 2000; Bennett 2012; Castells 2012; Dahlgren 2005; Loader & Mercea 2011; Warner 2002). Third, social media enables the autonomous construction of social networks controlled and managed by the users (Castells 2012). The users can seek, network, and consolidate with other like-minded people online to build digital communities and make their voices heard instantly through those networked communities (Lee et al. 2015).

In terms of social movements, social media largely reduces the limitations on public participation in the discussion on public issues. The easy access to social media gives every user an equal chance to speak. It also helps the activists to overcome, in the virtual world, the domination of the public sphere by those with power in the actual world (boyd 2010).[19] Furthermore, social media provides a new way to network in the global digital sphere. Activists who hold similar views and interests can network together without restrictions of time and space or distance, and so constitute various digital communities. Through free interaction within those communities, multiple digital public spheres can emerge (Squires 2002). Simultaneously, public opinions representative of those communities can be shared across online groups on social media (Lim 2017), increasing the possibility of gathering a larger, worldwide audience to join the discussions and mobilise for social movements (Castells 2009; Lee et al. 2015; Leung & Lee 2014; Palczewski 2001; Warner 2002).

Activists and social media use

In this section, I will develop on the ideas set out above and further explore the relationship between social media and its users in terms of the changes in communicative behaviours and networking and how these changes relate to current social movements. Firstly, I will use "prosumption theory" (Ritzer & Jurgenson 2010) to review what has changed when the users engage with social media and access the global digital sphere. Then, I will explore how users connect in current social

---

[19] Meyerhoff (2006) and Seargeant and Tagg (2013) assert that in online interpersonal relationships, personal contexts have been concealed by screens. Boyd (2010) also suggests "context collapse" to describe networked relationships on social media. She proposes that the users' demographic contexts in the actual world, such as career, education, income, are not important due to the lack of spatial, social and temporal boundaries in the virtual world.

movements through the notion of the "networked public" (boyd 2010).

The transformation of activists

When users browse stories and conversations on social media, they not only consume the content as audiences, but also 'produce' new content as producers.[20] Users create new posts, comment on the posts of others, or repost existing content to their own timelines. Similarly, uploading new videos and commenting on the videos of others are common production methods for users. Social media enables the public to collectively contribute to knowledge pooling and sharing (van Dijck 2013). This indicates that while social media facilitates the free and international transmission of information, it also enables users to create, develop and publish content and ideas online.

Ritzer and Jurgenson (2009; 2010) revive Alvin Toffler's idea of 'prosumption'[21]

---

[20] This idea develops upon the definition of communication as a two-way interactive process including the in and out information flows and the processes of coding and decoding (Jackson 2014; Fuchs 2017). However, Fuchs (2017) argues that tweeting, retweeting, commenting on Twitter are not communication because of the lack of explicit evidence of conversation. This thesis argues that while users produce content, share publicly and receive comments and retweets from the audiences, communication, in fact, has been achieved in this process.

[21] Alvin Toffler (1980) notes that the economic process of production and consumption are interrelated. The combination of production and consumption is prosumption. A prosumer is someone who is a producer and a consumer simultaneously.

(1980) and perceive users' behaviour on Web2.0 as a kind of presumption.[22] Furthermore, they stress this idea in the context of the global digital sphere. These scholars believe that when "there are speakers 'producing' talks, there is an audience 'consuming' them" somewhere (Ritzer, Dean & Jurgenson 2012, p. 387). And the audiences who consume the talks can produce their own responses. Thus, interaction on social media is truly a communication process in which participants actively both consume and produce ideas. Prosumption theory emphasises the active engagement of social media users, and indicates the impact of the content produced by an individual within a social network. Activists using social media, then, are content producers; and the audiences who consume their posts may, potentially, become activists themselves – when audiences respond publicly to the posts, this reaction can be seen by others within the social network and initiate another round of prosumption. Then, public opinion can be formed, modified, and shared widely and quickly in the virtual world.

The restructuring of social networks online

While social media reforms communication, scholars also believe that it impacts on the formation of social networks in the virtual world (Meyerhoff 2006; Seargeant &

---

[22] They point out that global connection of the Internet and Web 2.0 reflect the potential and will be the key to realising the idea of presumption. They start from the study of prosumer economy online. They highlight that in online business, consumers are more like workers since they need to start a self-service process to search a product, to evaluate it, to order it, and to pay for it. According to this stance, the concept of worker has been eliminated. Consumers unconsciously become the unpaid labours to produce "services" for their consumption (Ritzer 2015).

Tagg 2013). In particular, boyd (2010) suggests the idea of "networked public", and regards people on social media as an imagined collective (or community) constructed through networked technologies. Boyd (2010) emphasises that audiences in the networked publics are often invisible, their context are concealed[23] and the boundary between public and private lives blurs. When people use social media to mediate amongst themselves and to construct a networked public, they do so base on an agreement regarding shared interests and collective goals. In this online community, when individual users speak, they speak not only to their friends, but to the whole community. Fuchs (2017) criticises boyd for generalising the notion of the public to the whole realm of social media. However, I believe that the idea of the networked public will provide a new understanding of the relevance of the public sphere for current social movements.

Connecting the notions of activists as content producers and of the networked public, Papacharissi (2010) emphasises that social media empowers the voices of the activists by giving them greater autonomy, flexibility, and potential for political expression. She notes, also, like boyd, that social media collapses the boundaries between the

---

[23] According to Jackson's study (2014), the identity of an individual relates to how a person perceives himself and his own place in the world. Also, it is the basic concept that a person relies in order to identify which group or community he belongs to. Compared to the actual world where kinship and geographical links form the core of communities, shared interests and experiences become the core of online communities on social media (Meyerhoff 2006). Additionally, because of the lack of spatial, social and temporal boundaries in the virtual world, distinct social contexts of a person in the actual world are hard to maintain (boyd 2010). On social media, offline personal contexts collapse, and then the expression of identity will align with the online context (Wesch 2008).

private sphere and the political public sphere. This collapse gives even an individual activist the potential to guide public opinion (McGarty et al. 2014). In the reshaping of civic engagement on social media as a networked public, social capital is accumulated for further actions to address social issues (Warren et al. 2015).[24]

Fraser (1992) and Calhoun (1992) question Habermas's idea of the public sphere because it neglects the divergence of individual contexts and the heterogeneity of personal interests. However, I argue that by adding the 'networked public' to the 'public sphere', these shortcomings can be circumvented. Indeed, boyd (2010) and Papacharissi (2010) note that the public sphere is, in fact, located in various online communities constructed by people with different interests and goals. This is supported by Warner (2002) and Gerlach (2001) who speak about multiple publics that may become the centres, or hubs, for global activism in the age of ICTs. Developing upon Deleuze and Guattari's concept of the "rhizome"[25] (2004), Lim (2017) demonstrates that through social media, the multiple online networked publics have been connected and have become the "rhizomatic assemblage" for current social

---

[24] According to Social Capital theory (Coleman 1988; Nahapiet & Ghoshal 1998), actual and potential resources (social capital) can be obtained through the networks of social relationships among individuals. Social capital can be understood as structural, relational, and cognitive (Warren et al. 2015). On social media, when users are connected as networked publics and various online communities are formed to address social issues, the social capital can be understood as the relations of trust.

[25] Deleuze and Guattari (2004) suggests that online public can interact with one another by following the four principles of connectivity, heterogeneity, multiplicity and rupture and then become a rhizomatic structure. Online social platforms perform as "nodes" connecting different individuals and public. The nodes spread with no direction, with no beginning and no end.

movements. This is "a horizontal alliance with all the multiplicities that make a part of the rhizome interacting with one another" (Lim 2017, p. 211).[26] In other words, a many-to-many social structure has been built in the virtual world. This structure explains how social activism can 'diffuse' quickly through social media to become a global phenomenon,[27] and it points to the possibility of decentralised, personalised actions in social movements (Lee et al. 2017).

Social movements in the era of social media

Online activity energises disorganised crowds and/or facilitates the formation of networked publics around communities (Papacharissi 2014). The affordances of social media also enable expressions in information sharing that liberates individual and collective imaginations (boyd 2010). In this context, Castells (2012) and Bennett and Segerberg (2013) point out that the contemporary social movements are constructed by actions of a dispersed, decentralised, and hybrid character. Due to the development of social media and the interconnection provided by the Internet, online networks and the function of 'sharing' have become central to the distribution of information.

---

[26] The original sentence is linguistically odd. I take it to mean "a horizontal alliance with all the multiplicities that make parts of the rhizome interact with one another".

[27] Everett Rogers (2003) defines diffusion as "the process in which an innovation is communicated through certain channels over time among the members of a social system" (p. 5). Diffusion is a special type of communication which involves two or more individuals exchanging a new idea to achieve convergence or divergence.

Digital networks enable the emergence of a horizontal organisational structure and encourage individuals to contribute with their own deliberation. 'Connective actions', which emphasise the organisational power of networks, along with personal interests and expression, accompany digital technology in social movements. At the same time, the horizontal structure gradually diminishes the impact of the resource-rich hierarchical group in political actions. Organised groups are no longer the only actors in social movements; individuals who align with certain views on public issues and are connected through social media may now become active participants in social movements (Bennett & Segerberg 2013).

In conventional collective actions, activists gather together in a certain place and carry out a standardised action; today, however, people may also take part in a range of personalised or small-group based actions in other areas (Lee & Chan 2015). At the same time, indirect participation has become prevalent. Online action on social media – sharing onsite photos and protest posters; forming discussion groups to prepare slogans, strategies to counter public opinion, and protest plans; writing reports for foreign media – have become a significant part of participation in social movements (Lee & Chan 2015; Lim 2017).

Twitter /Facebook revolution?

Some scholars have argued that social media is not the cause of recent social movements (Olorunnisola & Martin 2014). I also believe that social media is a

communication tool and not the cause of social movements (Gladwell 2010;

Jurgenson 2012; Morozov 2011a; Rane & Salem 2012); rather, the climate of

frustration and the negative emotions shared among the public are the root cause of

the recent riots (Lee et al. 2017; Papacharissi 2014; Spilermen 1976; Tang 2015).

However, scholars have differing ideas on the role of social media in terms of

coordination, communication, and mobilisation in social movements.

Morozov (2011a) and Gladwell (2010) contest the claims that social media is

important for social movements. Morozov (2009) terms online activism

"slacktivism"[28], arguing that clicking 'like' and 'share' buttons, or joining a Facebook

group does not change anything in the actual world; the term "Twitter revolution"

only gives to the lazy generation an impractical illusion that they can achieve social

change by sitting in their bedrooms, typing on a keyboard, with no risk of arrest or of

being hurt (Morozov 2011a; 2011b). Gladwell (2010) concurs with Morozov's idea

and claims that people exaggerate the power and importance of social media in social

movements; for him, social media is not the natural enemy of the status quo.

Additionally, he claims that successful social movements need strong interpersonal

ties, a hierarchical structure, and the will to make a real sacrifice. These conditions

cannot be fulfilled by using social media, and thus, there is no "Twitter/Facebook

---

[28] Morozov (2009) defines the slacktivism is a type of feel-good online activism that has zero
political or social impact.

revolution" (Gladwell 2010). Ironically, Gladwell did not foresee the Arab Spring of 2011.

Castells (2012), however, argues that the Arab Spring and Occupy Wall Street (OWS) are significant examples of social movements involved in the construction of an autonomous space through combining physical space and the virtual world. In other words, the features of social media lead to a new form of social movement (Lee et al. 2017). To elaborate, social media activities constitute a significant part of the actions in current movements (Lee & Chan 2015). However, a mass of activists gathering in an actual place still matters, presenting a visible threat to those in power, in order to ultimately bring about material effects (Fuchs 2017). In current movements, such as Occupying Wall Street (OWS), Arab Spring, Hong Kong Umbrella Movement, Berish Movement, Taiwan Sunflower Movement, and Candlelight Movement in South Korea, activists embrace physical and digital protests simultaneously (Hui 2017; Jurgenson 2012; Lee 2017; Lim 2017; Wang 2017a).

Activists used social media to organise, record, speak, and share, but they are also willing to take over geographical spaces, mobilising physical bodies to yell, walk, sing, and even perhaps to fight against a police presence. Physical activities in protests cannot be replaced by virtual activities, but protestors' actions in the physical space are augmented by online participation (Hui 2017). Additionally, interpersonal relationships built in the virtual world can be actualised in the actual world through eye contact, communication of an emotional aura, and other bonding activities during

protests (Fuchs 2017). Seeing the two worlds as interlinked during protests, Jurgenson

(2012) concludes that it is incorrect to describe the current social movements as

"Twitter/Facebook revolution"; instead, they should be called "augmented

revolution". Against this background, I can assert that social media works as a

metaphorical 'bridge' connecting the virtual and actual worlds. Social media can

integrate public opinion and amplify its impact for social movements in both realms.

Social media and protest mobilisation

Activists' ability to use social media effectively gives rise to a new form of social

movement (Lee et al. 2017). It is interesting also to consider: how does social media

use mobilise potential activists to participate in social movements today?

Significantly, mobilisation also has a strong connection with the global digital sphere

and the networked public; the networked publics, access through social media, helps

activists to gather together grievances to mobilise potential activists to join their

movements.

Earl and Kimport (2011) point out that social media facilitates more powerful and

efficient mobilisation through building global digital connections. With social media

becoming an alternative source of news (Boykoff 2006), protesters equipped with

smartphones become journalists, and are able to record primary material from the protest sites and share this instantly and widely through social media (Jurgenson

2012). Thus, audiences online are more likely to encounter influential content, such as

confronting images that may trigger outrage and lead to participation (Forde 2011;

Leung & Lee 2014). The more the audiences are exposed to relevant messages of

protest, the more likely they are to be influenced (Nekmat 2012). Furthermore,

through social media, potential activists can connect directly with the activists onsite;

the activists' raw emotions can be mediated through narratives, such as posts, videos,

and photos (Tang 2015), and calls to action can be disseminated quickly from the

activists to the sympathetic networked public (Bennett & Segerberg 2013).

Social media can facilitate feelings of engagement through "affective content"[29]

shared with(in) the networked public (Dean 2010; van Dijck 2013; Gregg 2011;

Karatzogianni & Kuntsman 2012); these feelings can activate the latent ties of the

networked public that are crucial to the mobilisation in social movements

(Papacharissi 2014).[30] Additionally, the activists' statements and other content shared

with a networked public are persistent, replicable, scalable, and searchable, because

they have been recorded and archived on the servers (boyd 2010). The affective flow

and the links contributed by individual activists will remain and resonate with the

---

[29] Papacharissi (2014) defines this word as the content with "affect". It is the sum of discordant feelings about public and private affairs.

[30] Papacharissi refers the "latent ties" to the similarity of identities (e.g. black people), awareness of existing problems (e.g. injustice in law), the feeling of belonging and solidarity as a community (e.g. brothers and sisters) and the common-agreed goals of a protest (e.g. looking for equality).

networked public, even after the specific links to content have been shut down (Dean

2010). In other words, the power to mobilise, inherent in affective content shared

among a networked public, will persist for a long time. The content will "reflexively

drive a movement that aims at community and/or capture users in a state of engaged

passivity" (Papacharissi 2014, p. 10).

Trust in information shared through social media is another issue in relation to social

movement mobilisation. For Warren et al. (2015), trust is part of the social capital that

can be derived from ties of social interaction. Strong interpersonal networks, like

friends and family members, will encourage the extension of an invitation to

participate and ease the uncertainty of mobilisation (Gladwell 2010; McAdam &

Paulsen 1993). Even weak social ties among strangers, such as between members of

an online photography group, still have a significant impact on online participatory

behaviours (Chiu et al. 2006). Rheingold (2002) borrows insights from marketing and

points out that when an individual constantly invests time and contributes intelligent

resources to the network, she or he will earn a positive reputation and become an

opinion leader. Moreover, trust in the era of social media can be merely a quantitative

concept. According to van Dijck's research (2013), many social media accounts are

followed because they are recognised as popular, and so other users want to connect

with them too. This quantifiable value is touted, and, for those other users/followers,

builds the reputation and "famous" images of the owner of the popular account (van

Dijck 2013); that is why online 'celebrities' have the power to motivate a large number of followers to act.

With the increasing involvement of social media use in contemporary social movements, the costs of participating in the digital public sphere have decreased; people in the digital sphere are connected according to their networks on social media and are easily affected and mobilised through expressions of emotions and opinions. The digital public sphere, in fact, has provided a rich ground for social capital pooling and information sharing for recent social movements. Social media use is interwoven with the change in protest actions in both the physical and digital worlds, and social movements today seem to be duplicable from one place to another through social media. Together, these circumstances suggest that contemporary social movements are indeed becoming augmented.

Chapter 1 Social Movements in Arab and Hong Kong

The Arab Spring has been discussed frequently in the past few years in terms of its

political effects but also in relation to the significant changes in the use of social

media during the protests. This event attracted global attention because it encouraged

local and international citizens to contribute to the protests and, especially, because it

led to the dramatic end of the ruling regimes of Ben Ali in Tunisia and Hosni

Mubarak in Egypt (Carty 2015). Social media figured strongly, performing as an

efficient channel of mediation, forming a digital public sphere for the bringing

together and airing of grievances, and supporting instant exchange of information

within and between networks, domestically and internationally (Bennett 2012;

Bennett & Segerberg 2013; Castell 2012; Rane & Salem 2012).

These protests were recognised as unconventional movements: the main collective

protest action employed was the occupation of symbolic physical spaces, such as,

Bourguiba Avenue in Tunisia and Tahrir Square in Egypt (AlSayyad & Guvenc 2013),

but, at the same time, the participants relied heavily on social media to organise,

coordinate, and mobilise through their networks (Bennett & Segerberg 2013). With

the help of social media, the protests "scaled up very quickly, had a decentralized

formation, and…the (political) organisations did not play a strong leadership role"

(Lee 2015, p. 333). Also, a wide range of spontaneous small-group and individual

actions emerged during the movements (Lee 2015). Through social media, practical strategies in relation to how to effectively occupy and demonstrate, how to fight

against repressive authorities, as well as how to protect oneself from the effects of tear

gas were shared across national borders from Tunisia, to Egypt, to other battlefields in

the Middle East and North Africa (MENA) region (Buhler-Muller & van der Merwe

2011).

Later, some scholars also demonstrated that the Arad Spring, and especially the

protests in Egypt, enlightened, to a greater or lesser degree, the later Occupy

Movements around the world (Castells 2012; Highfield 2016; Lee & Chan 2015;

Papacharissi 2014). In particular, the most famous protest of the Occupy Movements,

well known as the Occupy Wall Street (OWS), erupted at the legendary financial

centre of the world in New York. It has been observed that this protest shared many

characteristics with the Arab Spring (Bennett 2012; Bennett & Segerberg 2013;

Castell 2012; Rane & Salem 2012; Skinner 2011). The activists were summoned

mainly through Twitter and Facebook, and then flowed into and blocked Zuccotti

Park close to Wall Street, in September 2011(Suh et al. 2017).

Interestingly, the Hong Kong Umbrella Movement of 2014, was, in its early stages,

recognised as Occupy Central or Occupy Central with Love and Peace(OCLP) (Yuen

2015).[31] The Umbrella Movement was implicitly defined as a kind of the Occupy

Movement by its adoption of the obvious stamp 'occupy', and by its main feature, the

occupation of the most important business and political centres of Hong Kong (Huat

2017). Indeed, recent research has shown that three main districts of business and

finance in Hong Kong – firstly Admiralty, and then Mong Kok and Causeway Bay –

were flooded by the activists during the Umbrella Movement (Lee 2015; Lee & Ting

2015; Lee et al. 2015). Facebook, the most popular social networking sites (SNSs) in

Hong Kong, was adopted to obtain and spread news, promote the movement, and

attract potential activists to join in the occupation (Lee et al. 2015).

Above all, social movements today have shown that physical protest actions cannot be

discussed separately from social media in relation to connecting the protestors onsite

and the onlookers or potential supporters online. Furthermore, there is a notable trend

toward social media's deep involvement in social movements through providing

alternative access to information and to various massive networks in the virtual world.

For instance, in Egypt, regarding situations that did not receive coverage by the state-

controlled news, information could be gathered by accessing the photos and videos

shared directly from the protesters in Tahrir Square, through Facebook and Twitter

---

[31] This idea was proposed by Benny Tai, a law professor in University of Hong Kong and the agitator of Occupy Central. He suggested that Hong Kong citizens should have a large-scale civil disobedience to fight for their right of universal suffrage for the election of the chief executive of Hong Kong. He absorbed the ideas of "rational" and "non-violent" from the Occupy Movements and encouraged the citizens to sit-in peacefully on a major road in Central, Hong Kong (Yuen 2015).

(Carty 2015). In addition, considering boyd's networked public (2010), the messages that are shared through social media do not just shout into the wind, but to the audience network, with instantaneous connection and unconstrained by geographical boundary – someone next door or on the other side of the planet will be reached simultaneously.

With the intense engagement of social media, social movements are no longer just in the hands of politicians, parties, or political organisations. Instead, average citizens can express their views online and turn their Facebook and Twitter friends into companions in the movements. In the Tunisian uprising, the self-immolation of Mohamed Bouazizi was captured by Ali Bouazizi (Mohamed Bouazizi's distant cousin) in photos. He wrote an impressive story of sorrow to accompany the image and shared these through his Facebook page. The story was quickly reposted and the augmented circulation awakened the Arab world (Lim 2013).

Although the Arab Spring and the Hong Kong Umbrella Movement demonstrate some explicit similarities, these two movements did not happen under similar cultural, political and economic background, nor did they pursue the same goal. On one hand, during the Arab Spring, many of the countries in the MENA region were under the jurisdiction of religious doctrines, such as Muslim and Christian (Frangonikoloppoulos & Chapsos 2012). Also in some of these countries, such as Tunisia and Egypt, the ruling regimes had been controlled for decades by dictators "without transparency and with little respect for rule of law, civil right, or the formal realm of political process" (Carty 2015, p. 87). Corruptions, violent abuse by the government, high unemployment rates, poverty, and the lack of freedom of speech and democratic and human rights were common and serious concerns under those dictatorships (Lim 2013). Therefore, in order to achieve significant change of the situation, the activists in Tunisia and Egypt desired, through the uprisings, to overthrow the governments as well as remove their pitiless leaders (Rane & Salem 2012).

Hong Kong, on the other hand, is a former British colony and adopted the Western capitalist economic system following colonisation. The economic system was guaranteed to be maintained for the next 50 years after the colony's handover to China in 1997, under the statement of "One Country, Two Systems" in the *Sino-British Joint Declaration* of 1984. Additionally, in order to promote democracy, the National People's Congress (NPC) decided to introduce universal suffrage for the election of the Chief Executive of Hong Kong by 2017 (Yuen 2015). However, the universal suffrage declared by the NPC was different from that expected by the citizens, and Occupy Central, which evolved into the 79 days long Umbrella

Movement, was set against 'fake universal suffrage'.[32]

Unlike the Arab Spring, instead of aiming to subvert the whole ruling regime, the Umbrella Movement targeted no more than a policy which was recognised as unfair (Lee et al. 2015). While the people in the MENA countries have experienced massive regression and violence from their governments, Hong Kong has a relatively democratic history, and a prosperous economy, and enjoys more freedom of speech – even though it is now being squeezed under the government of China (Lim 2013; Tsui 2015). Besides, Hong Kong is a developed international city with well-established ICT infrastructures: according to previous studies, Hong Kong has a high rate of mobile phone coverage (about 241.7 per cent) and household broadband coverage (about 83.2 per cent) (Tsui 2015). Facebook is the dominant platform of social media used in Hong Kong (Fu & Chan 2015), with – up to 2014 – a coverage rate of nearly 67.22 per cent (Economy Watch 2015); around 4.4 million people in Hong Kong were Facebook users by 2014 (Lam 2014). In the MENA region, at the end of 2010, there were about 20 million Facebook users. However, the average national coverage rate of Facebook was only 7 per cent; specifically, the rate was 18 per cent in Tunisia, 5 per cent in Egypt, 4 per cent in Libya, and only 1 per cent in both Syria and Yemen (Salem & Mourtada 2011). Furthermore, it is notable that 75 per cent of the Facebook

---

[32] According to Yuen (2015), the NPC declared that universal suffrage in Hong Kong is a public vote for candidates that selected by the NPC, rather than a public nomination of candidates. Thus, some citizens critiqued that this is a "fake universal suffrage" since their available choices have been regulated and limited by the NPC.

users in this region were in the 15 to 29 years age group (Frangonikoloppoulos & Chapsos 2012), whereas in Hong Kong, the major group of Facebook users were aged from 18 to 34 years (Lam 2014).

According to the data above, there is a big difference between Hong Kong and the countries in the MENA region in terms of political, economic, and cultural context, and in the development of ICT infrastructures, as well as a difference in the goals set by their respective movements. However, the active use of social media to network, obtain news, express ideas, and spread information during the protests is a feature common to both movements (Ahy 2016; Frangonikoloppoulos & Chapsos 2012; Lin 2017; Tang 2015). These findings imply that the national rate of social media coverage is not the vital determinant for sustaining the momentum of social movements; rather, what is vital is the awareness of social media and ability to adopt it for a specific purpose. The data also indicate that it was the younger generation that was the major group that enthusiastically participating in the movements via social media. The youths were well-equipped with media-making skills, and able to use social media as a tool to observe and mediate the world, voice their opinions and take political action (Lee & Ting 2015). To elaborate, Joshua Wong's student activist group, Scholarism, is a remarkable and influential group of experienced Hong Kong teenagers, who skilfully used social media to speak, mobilise and guide public opinion not only in the 2014 Umbrella Movement, but also in the Anti-Moral and

National Education movement (Anti-M&N) in 2012 (Wang 2017b).[33] Friedman

(2014) regards those young activists as "square people", he points out that, via social

media, young people can connect to one another by gathering either in physical

spaces or virtual space.

Friedman's statement about square people will help to bring the hypothesis of

augmented reality back to the role of social media: his statement is in line with my

assumption, through his emphasis on the simultaneity of the virtual and the actual

worlds and the active role of the young social media users in both dimensions. Some

previous studies also suggest relevant ideas that support this hypothesis. For example,

Scott McQuire (2006) remarks that the public domain in the twenty-first century

cannot be understood simply as material structures, such as streets and plazas; the

overlapping of virtual networks onto the territorial space of cities has generated a new

"hybrid" form of space. Castells (2012) emphasises that social media is involved in

the construction of a "space of autonomy" for social movements by integrating urban

---

[33] The Anti-Moral and National Education (Anti-M&N) movement in 2012 targeted the
announcement of the Hong Kong Chief Executive which claimed that in order to cultivate the
national identity of Hong Kong students, "moral and national education" (M&N) would be taught
as an independent subject in every primary and secondary school. Joshua Wong and his
Scholarism, which mainly constructed by high school students, suggested that the M&N in fact
exalts the Chinese Communities Party and will "brainwash" Hong Kong's next generation. They
stood up to fight against the decision of the government and launched a hunger strike and
"Occupy Government Headquarters" (later was recognised as "Occupy Civic Square"). Through
starting group discussion, building alliances with other organisations and sharing the activities and
the statements of the students on Facebook, Joshua and his group successfully attracted thousands
of participants to join the occupation and finally made the government to terminate the program
(Wang 2017b). The training and lessons learned in this movement also equipped and enhanced the
Scholarism with sophisticated communication and large-scale movement organisation capabilities
for the Umbrella Movement in 2014 (Wong 2015, Lee & Ting 2015).

space with cyberspace. Jurgenson (2012) further develops these ideas in his discussion of the concept of "augmented reality", arguing that social media augments our offline lives instead of replacing them: online and offline are not separate spheres; they are interrelated and one can be used to bolster the other. Jurgenson also demonstrates that our friends on Facebook commonly derive from our offline contacts. At the same time, on social media, users are trained to experience the actual world "as a potential photo, tweet, check-in, or status-update" (Jurgenson 2012, p. 85). Recently, Lin (2017) observed social media repertoires notes that when people "unfriend" a friend with a different political opinion on Facebook, it is likely that they unfriend the same one in the actual world – evidence that our online activities will also influence our decision-making in the actual world.

These ideas propose that the virtual and actual worlds come together through social media to form an augmented reality. At the intersection of the actual and the virtual worlds, social media, as a 'bridge' enables its users to mediate the actual world towards the virtual dimension through various materials and, conversely, allows what has been mediated online to affect users' offline lives. Social media provides a means for activists to actively promote social movements through the virtual networks, and participate in collective and connective actions by making the protests virtual while the grievances are actual. From this viewpoint, this thesis argues that the Arab Spring and the Umbrella Movement are "augmented revolutions". Social media not only helps these movements to extend from the physical domain to the digital domain and go global through producing and sharing posts, but also restructures physical space by actualising online networks in the movements.

Chapter 2 Virtualising the Actual World

In augmented reality, there are two directions of information flow: from offline to online, and from online to offline. These two dimensions are interactive: what we experience in the actual world will influence what we share and how we act in the virtual world, and vice versa. Through their embeddedness in social media, the Arab Spring and the Umbrella Movement take the form of 'augmented revolutions'.

In this chapter, I argue that social media, in augmented revolutions, helped these social movements to extend from the physical domain to the digital domain and to spread from local to global contexts. In this process, the private content on Facebook gradually became an alternative source of protest related information for onlookers and even mainstream media. When uploading this information, the activists applied framing in preparing their posts in order to stress their viewpoints and invoke outrage online, which then led to mobilising actions in the actual world. In this way, "rhizomatic assemblages" in the virtual world become the core structure for information diffusion in ongoing movements.

In particular, this thesis will analyse the public posts shared by influential Facebook accounts, such as 'We are all Khaled Said', Scholarism, and Joshua Wong, during the movements. These posts have multiple likes, comments, and reposts, and at the same time, they indicate the process of mediating the actual movements to the virtual world. This makes them particularly interesting and useful for my analysis. Some

posts under these accounts were already removed from Facebook on the date of

writing, and they only can be tracked through previous studies. In order to

demonstrate the diversity of mediation and framing of the activists, some less widely

disseminated posted by ordinary users will be discussed as well.

Breaking the boundaries

Although the activists of the Arab Spring and the Umbrella Movement relied heavily

on social media (Chan & Lee 2014; Frangonikoloppoulos & Chapsos 2012; Lee &

Ting 2015), research reveals that traditional news channels, such as satellite and cable

television, as well as mobile phone messages, also played important roles in

motivating audiences and spreading the movements (Bruns et al. 2013; Lin 2017).

These studies also indicate that international mainstream media today increasingly

value posts on social media. By using the online posts as a part of their news

broadcasting, mainstream media have built a link to social media.

Ahy (2016) suggests that the Arab Spring and the Umbrella Movement are examples

of "transmedia" or networked multimedia communication. In line of Papacharissi's

consideration of the blurring of the boundary between the public and private spheres

in the digital era (2010), I suggest that in the process of transmedia networking, the

boundary between formal news (public) and personal posts (private) has been blurred.

Through international broadcasts, local events spread across national borders, and then increased awareness of the movements among audiences in other regions.

Mass media still had some authority over news communication in both movements for several reasons. First, mass media cannot be completely replaced by social media, due to the limited reliability of online posts (Ahy 2016). Second, social movements need mass media to vindicate their causes (Gamson & Wolfsfeld 1993). Third, according to demographic data, there is still a larger number of people, especially among the older generation, who do not use social media as their news source, or rarely use it (Lee & Ting 2015; Lee et al. 2015).

In Hong Kong, most people in the older age groups still regard mass media as the trustworthy news source (Lee et al. 2015). Also, according to a survey of the media preferences of Hong Kong citizens (So 2014), 52 per cent of Hong Kong citizens regard television as the major source of political information, while 27.3 per cent of them rely on newspapers. In other words, the traditional news channels in Hong Kong still hold the authority (Chan & Lee 2007; Lee & Chan 2011); specifically, TVB (the major television broadcasting media), *Ming Pao* and *Apple Daily* (newspapers) still have large audiences and readership today (Tang 2015).

Similarly, in Tunisia and Egypt, at the beginning of the movements there, television was regarded as the major source for obtaining updates regarding the protests (Ahy 2016). However, this might be attributable more to the low rate of Internet and social

53

media coverage, as mentioned above. Additionally, domestic news media were mainly supervised and controlled by the state. For example, Ben Ali's family owned four newspapers in Tunisia and controlled the major news outlets in the early stage of the uprising (Carty 2015); protest related information would not be distributed to audiences through these channels (Frangonikoloppoulos & Chapsos 2012). The local audiences counted more on international mainstream media, such as Al Jazeera[34], CNN, and BBC, for receiving credible political information (van Leuven et al. 2013).

However, mainstream media have shortcomings too. During the Arab Spring and the Umbrella Movement, the credibility and accessibility of mainstream media were suspected. On one hand, in Tunisia and Egypt, in order to suppress the growing protests, the governments of these countries struck at the mainstream media (Carty 2015). While the Tunisian government applied strong censorship to newscasts and blocked the broadcasting sites of Al Jazeera, in Egypt, the Mubarak regime even eliminated Al Jazeera's government controlled satellite, dismissed its bureau, seized its transmission equipment, and arrested its journalists and staff (Carty 2015).[35] The traditional processes of news production and distribution were severely undermined

---

[34] Al Jazeera is an Arabic news outlet that relatively independent from the ruling regimes in the MENA region. It is highly respected for its inclusion of different perspectives on reporting sensitive regional and global issues. It works as an alternative news source other than the state-controlled media that could be accessed by many countries in the Arab world (Whitaker 2003).

[35] Carty cites a news article by Karr and Le Coz (2011), 'How Western Corporations Have Been Helping Tyrants Suppress Rebellion in the Arab World' on *AlterNet*. However, the link to the article is no longer available.

by those with political power.

On the other hand, the local mainstream media in Hong Kong tended to self-censor in their news production in order to cull sensitive messages, and intrinsic bias, according to the owners' political background, was embedded in their reporting on social issues (Tang 2015; Tsui 2015). In particular, TVB was regarded as a monopolistic and politically conservative broadcaster, and *Apple Daily* was well known as a newspaper of the pro-democracy camp (Lee 2015a; Lee & Chan 2008). As Noam Chomsky cautions (2002), the ownership of the media leads to an imbalance in political opinion. In this situation, social media can be understood as a supplementary news outlet for the mainstream media, offering both raw materials and an instantaneous means of distribution, which is difficult to censor. Social media also provides activists with a forum to directly deliver their own opinions and reframe their movements. Above all, in augmented revolutions, activists enjoy more freedom of expression online; at the same time, mainstream media can overcome the restrictions of governments through their virtual connections to the activists on social media.

It is worth focusing now on how social media, such as Facebook or Twitter, become news channels. Or, what can activists do with social media to aid social movements? In the Arab Spring, the rate of coverage for Facebook being relatively low in the MENA region (Salem & Mourtada 2011), it was difficult for activists to disseminate messages widely by relying on a single platform. In order to boost the effectiveness of

55

dissemination, it was reasonable to connect one platform to another and so reach a larger audience. This study finds that the activists also accessed to mainstream media by using social media.

Following boyd (2010), networked technologies, or social media in this case, introduce new affordances to their users in terms of recording, amplifying, and spreading information and social actions based on social media's ability to persist, replicate, scale, and search. According to boyd (2010), persistence refers to the archiving function on social media; replicability means that online content can be duplicated; scalability emphasises that large potential audiences exist within a network; searchability indicates that the content shared within networked publics can be searched through search functions on social media platforms. The concept of "produser" or "prosumer" in the social media scene indicates that the activists are encouraged to generate original posts and feedback (Bruns 2008; Ritzer & Jurgenson 2010). Together, activists can record what happens in the actual world and then share this record online. The facts of the movements are captured in fragments by mobile phones and cameras. Through social media, these materials are archived online and ready for reposting and subsequent searching (if the content can be seen by the public). For instance, the image of Tahrir Square in *figure 1* was derived directly from the protesting site. It was posted on 9 July 2011 and can be searched and found to this day. It captures a scene of the rally on that day.

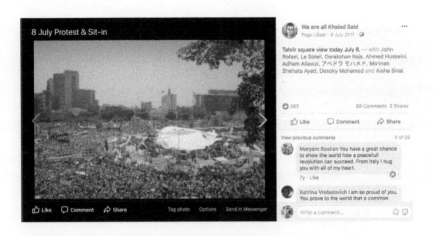

(Figure 1: A photo of the Egypt uprising in Tahrir Square on Facebook. Viewed on 31

July 2018)

Social media amplifies the voices of the activists, and so empowers them, through

boosting the popularity of individual posts in connection with the movements.

According to van Dijck (2013), the number of 'likes' and followers of an account's

posts on social media is viewed as a visible and countable indicator for evaluating the

popularity of that account.[36] This popularity principle is applicable to the analyse of a

post as well: clicking the 'like' button generates an affective bond between the

---

[36] Van Dijck (2013) notes that unlike in the offline world where people are "well-connected", online social activities are translated into algorithmic concepts because of the weak ties online and the abnormally large number of contacts. "Friends" and "Followers" can be interpreted under the popularity principle which means that the more contacts a person has on social media, the more valuable, popular and authoritative they become and hence other people want to connect with them. She also suggests that "likability is not a virtue attributed consciously by a person to a thing or idea, but is the result of an algorithmic computation derived from instant clicks on the Like button" (p. 14). Although the Like button does not include any quality assessment, in the online economy of social media, it is an important quantitative concept to evaluate the popularity of ideas. The more Likes an idea receives, the more likely the idea becomes a trend and is promoted as a topic with high popularity ranking by the system.

activists and their audiences. Other research (Wang et al. 2017) suggests that the higher the number of 'likes' a Facebook post attracts, the more engagement may be triggered between the reader and the content. Also, based on the Facebook algorithm, the more 'likes' a post receives, the more probable it is that the post will be seen by other Facebook users (van Dijck 2013) – when an individual sees that a friend 'likes' a post on Facebook, he or she may 'like' it too (Gerlitz & Helmond 2013), and the number of 'likes' will increase the momentum for information circulation. From this perspective, Facebook is helping activists to establish and reach broader audiences for what is happening in their movements.

Above all, the activists have become "citizen journalists" who mediate their protests in the actual world through social media (Lim 2013). The content of their posts are open for searching and reposting; consequently, individual posts become fragments of the whole picture of the movements and may serve as an item of news. Through different angles of narrative and interpretation, more information is added to the news story given out by the mainstream media. In this sense, the actual world is virtualised in the process of posting on social media. Local issues become borderless when they enter the virtual world. The first path for social movements to become augmented has been paved.

The role of activists on social media becomes more vital when international mainstream media are not granted access to local sources. According to research on the Arab Spring, there was a clear trend that the information flowed from social media

content creators to professional journalists (Ahy 2016). Particularly in the Egyptian

and Tunisian uprisings, heavy media restrictions were imposed on the international

mainstream media, and the journalists in these media – such as CNN, BBC, and Al

Jazeera – were forced to refer to non-authoritative sources, which includes social

media content (van Leuven et al. 2015). It has been shown that Al Jazeera absorbed

the immolation images and videos posted by Ali Bouazizi on Facebook to prepare its

first reportages, as well as using citizen videos from YouTube to disclose the Tunisian

uprising (Lim 2013).

Meanwhile, the Internet block was imposed by governments in order to suppress

social media use during the movements. This restriction was circumvented by using

"Voice2Tweet" (Bruns et al. 2013). This tool was announced by Google and Twitter,

and enabled the activists in the MENA region to keep connecting on Twitter by

making international phone calls and leaving voice messages (Rane & Salem 2012;

Zuckerman 2011). Consequently, news materials were transferred from local private

sources to public social platforms, like Twitter, and were ready to be absorbed by the

international media.

In Hong Kong, the use of social media to record the Umbrella Movement was similar

to that in the Arab Spring (see e.g. *figure 2*). Also, as shown in *figure 3*, *Apple Daily*

retrieved a video from a protestor to report the conflict between the protesters and police and reveal how the police used pepper spray to dismiss the crowd. This was a

valuable piece of news that the journalists of the newspaper may not easily have

obtained from the front line of the protest, due to their limited manpower and the

abruptness of the incident.

(Figure 2: Two girls having a rest at one of the occupied main roads on the protest

site. Viewed on 7 August 2018)

(Figure 3: *Apple Daily* referred to a video from a protestor in its social media post.

Viewed 7 August 2018)

It is important to note that in both cases mainstream media could access these news materials when incidents were virtualised through social media. However, compared with the uprisings in the MENA region, a clearer awareness and a planned strategy of using social media to mediate the protests and influence mainstream media can be observed in the Umbrella Movement (Ahy 2016; Highfield 2016; Lee & Ting 2015; Wang 2017b; Lin 2017). The most salient example is Joshua Wong's and Scholarism's media strategy. During the Umbrella Movement, the young activists developed the concept of "we media" to deliver the Umbrella Movement's political discourse and mission (Lee & Ting 2015). In his book (2014), Joshua Wong also stresses that he realised the importance of approaching mainstream media to enhance the influence of the movement, rather than relying only on social media. The group therefore created official pages on Facebook to interact directly with the public, and, at the same time, worked closely with mainstream media.[37] In both cases, despite the activists using social media to actively or passively contact mainstream media, their political discourses were finally adopted by mainstream media and reshaped public opinion on

---

[37] It is legitimate to ask if mainstream media belong to the virtual world. Given that mainstream media own their websites and social media accounts, they also exist in the virtual world and transfer news from the offline world to online world. The difference to individual accounts on social media is that content production is supervised by corporations and the information flow is determined within the hierarchical structure of the corporations.

a wider range.

The major channels for the protestors were the official Facebook pages of Scholarism (which received about 310,000 'likes'), *Dash*[38] (which received about 100,000 'likes'), and the Facebook page of Joshua Wong (Chan & Fu 2014). Through those popular social media pages, not only the protest actions were demonstrated online, but the young activists could also directly convey their opinions to the participants of the movements and to the general public, thus avoiding misinterpretation and misinformation associated with the government controlled media. In turn, the exclusive information on those pages had a strong influence on the mainstream media, since journalists needed to visit these websites and platforms for accurate and current news (Lee & Ting 2015).

The members of Scholarism were also well trained to deal with press interviews, deliver public speeches, write press releases, prepare press conferences, and decide when to provide exclusive reports to certain media and when to make appeals to all media. Also, these young activists were able to create unorthodox media events and scenarios to attract mainstream media's attention (Lin 2017). In this way, not only did Joshua Wong and his fellows become media attractions (see also *figure 4*), but they

---

[38] *Dash* is a student publication developed and led by Joshua Wong, and run by the members of Scholarism after the Anti-Moral and National Education (Anti-M&N) movement in 2012, Hong Kong (Lee & Ting 2015, about Anti-M&N movement see also footnote in Chapter 1). *Dash* was used to post the youngsters' (secondary high school students) viewpoints on civil society during the Umbrella Movement.

also controlled news resources and shaped public opinion through mainstream media.

For example, when the Education authority criticised the boycott of classes,

Scholarism posted on its Facebook page numerous speeches by university professors

and celebrities declaring the movement as a symbolic and exciting moment for Hong

Kong citizens fighting for democracy. This viewpoint was also conveyed to the public

through mainstream media, such as *South China Morning Post*, *Apple Daily*, *Radio

Television Hong Kong (RTHK)*, *CNN*, *BBC*, *Al Jazeera*, and subsequently gained

attention from both domestic and international societies (*Joshua: Teenager vs.

Superpower* 2017; Lee & Ting 2015; Lin 2017).

(Figure 4: Joshua Wong appears on the cover of the *TIME* magazine. Viewed 9
August 2018)

Consequently, the social movements became "transmedia", emphasising the

63

transferral from a private dimension to a public one. Individual protestors became more influential in the public discourse through the mainstream media. Furthermore, as personal posts were absorbed by the international media, the social movements could be shown to a larger range of audiences, regardless of the geographical or political borders. Therefore, augmented revolutions break not only the boundary between private and public, but also the boundary between time and space.

Interestingly, I found that in contrast to that in Hong Kong, the transmedia process in the MENA region was more passive. In Hong Kong, the protestors intentionally included the mainstream media as a part of their operational strategy, while in the MENA countries, the international mainstream media came to the protestors for news when they were banned by the government. Also, the Umbrella Movement had Joshua Wong as its iconic leader, although his leadership is still a controversial topic (Lee 2015b; Lin 2017; Yates, 2015). However, there was no official leadership during the uprisings in the Arab Spring (Lim 2017), and so clear and organised transmedia strategies could not be devised. Poell and Darmoni (2012) argue that their using English, the international lingua franca, rather than Arabic in the process of virtualising the Arab Spring is evidence of the activists communicating with the West to gain global attention. However, this does not prove that the activists intended to include the mainstream media in their operational strategy.

Truth or 'white lies'?

Becoming citizen journalists, the activists had more scope to frame their reportage when mediating the protests. I believe that the use of framing in the process of virtualising the Arab Spring and the Umbrella Movement helped to summon supporters in the virtual world, and consequently to translate the local issues into an international topic. In particular, scholars emphasise that activists use framing to give more meanings and purpose to their actions, and set goals beyond the actions themselves to become a part of "something bigger" (Gamson et al. 1982; Snow et al. 1986; Tarrow 1998). At the same time, they use framing to define the central values of their cause, that legitimate the protests, as well as to proclaim the motivation, the grievances and demands giving rise to the movement, and to build a bridge from themselves to their potential audiences (Carty 2015; Givan et al. 2010; Snow et al. 1986; Soule 2004). Rane and Salem (2012) also assert that framing is an issue closely associated with the leadership and the audiences of a social movement. Unlike framing in mainstream media, where vision is limited by factors such as profit, sources, and the owner's political position, the citizen journalists' framing provides more direct, diverse, and realistic viewpoints for their audiences. Thus, framing provides freedom for activists to negotiate the reason for actions with their audiences in augmented revolutions.

The term "frame" was first suggested by Goffman (1974, p. 21) as the "schemata of interpretation". He proposed that frames allow individuals to "locate, perceive, identify, and label" information actively, and make sense of it according to their own life experience. Pan and Kosicki (1993) state that a frame is a cluster of data and words, constructed by various pieces of organised, identical and cognitive information in the psychological conception. It could be interpreted with different meanings and absorbed into different perceptions by audiences, and then arouse various emotions affecting their behaviours (Boulding 1959). Journalists use framing to package information and effectively guide public opinion among their audiences (Gitlin 1980). In order to interpret and analyse the framing of the citizen journalists on social media and their effects during the movements, framing analysis (Pan & Kosicki 1993) will be applied here.

In particular, Mohamed Bouazizi's dramatic self-immolation is well known as the trigger for the Tunisian uprising in the Arab Spring (Carty 2015; Howard & Hussain 2013; Rane & Salem 2012). This was a shocking and sorrowful way to end one person's life and a tragedy for the whole country. It is believed that the impact of this news was strong enough to provoke outrage across the country and ignite the protests. However, Lim (2013) argues that Mohamed Bouazizi's was not the first self-suicide in a public venues in Tunisia.[39] So, why did Bouazizi's death successfully trigger the

---

[39] In fact, another street vendor, Abdesslem Trimech, set himself on fire just a few months before the uprising broke out because of the similar reason to Bouazizi's. Trimech was one of nine self-immolations in the six months leading up to Bouazizi's death. Yet, the death of Trimech and other martyrs merely sparked small local protests and failed to inspire massive actions (Lim 2013).

uprising, rather than others? This thesis believes that the framing of Bouazizi's story amplified its effects. At the same time, by bringing Bouaziz's story to the virtual world, the crimes of Ben Ali's regime were exposed to a wider range of online audiences; the increasing grievance and fury of the audiences will become the seedbed for further protest actions.

Lim (2012; 2013) makes two important suggestions in response to this question: first, witnesses used mobile phones to record the tragedy and then disseminated the horrifying news online; and second, Bouazizi's story itself played a vital role in the revolt. The frames of the story were greater than the death itself, and they resonated with the people who were struggling, culturally and emotionally, under Ben Ali's regime.

When Mohamed set himself on fire, his cousin, Ali Bouazizi, was the first to capture photos of his burning body and the ensuing protest on his mobile phone, and distribute them to Facebook (Arab Centre for Research and Policy Studies 2011). Ali Bouazizi quickly recognised the importance of framing around the images (Lim 2013). As Lim (2013) points out, one of the reasons that the previous self-immolations did not trigger the uprising is that they were considered foolish actions. So, in order to make Mohamed's death matter, Ali gave his cousin's burning body a compelling story:

> Firstly, Ali framed (Mohamed) Bouazizi…as an unemployed

university graduate who turned to sell produce to make ends
meet…Secondly, he inserted a 'slap in the face' by Fedia Hamdi, an
authority who is also a woman, and made it central to the story of
Bouazizi's public humiliation (Lim 2013, p. 927).

Through this frame, Ali tried to make Mohamed's death a reminder of the high

unemployment rate and poor life prospects among educated youths under Ben Ali's

regime. Lim (2013) also mentions that for a woman to slap a man in the face is a

taboo in Arab cultures. The woman in question was a government officer, so this slap

was actually a slap from the authorities in the face of the customs of the country, and

this would provoke fury among the traditional public. Furthermore, before

Mohamed's self-immolation, he was beaten by police officers in the street, simply

because he lacked money to pay for the "permit" to sell fruits, or, precisely, to bribe a

local official (Schroeder et al. 2014). When the "slap" was discussed in the virtual

domain, it would recall and amplify the violence that the police inflicted on Mohamed

and associated this story with the corruption and the pitilessness of Ben Ali's

government. Under the cruel ruling of the government, Mohamed's social and

political rights were denied and he finally sacrificed himself to reclaim justice, his

dignity and freedom (Rane & Salem 2012). Through this frame, Mohamed became a

symbol for the rebellion in pursuit of those noble values for the country.

The framing of Mohamed is also positioned within the concept of frame bridging and frame amplification (Snow et al. 1986)[40]: scholars believe that frames can build

connections between two or more individuals or groups if they are ideologically

relevant regarding a particular issue, and pursuing similar values and beliefs, such as

justice, equality, and liberty. Mohamed's story and image resonated with those

frustrated people who recognised themselves as being poor and suffering, or

unemployed, or simply young, or as having been insulted, or as feeling dissatisfied

with the government. Thus, the protests for Mohamed were able to motivate people

across classes and diverse social groups, not only in his own town, but also across

Tunisia, and finally resonating with the wider Arab world through social media.

Once frames had been established, they could be duplicated and spread from one

movement to another (Schroeder et al. 2014). Through social media, this transmission

could be fast and wide. Rane and Salem (2012) suggest that social media indeed

facilitated a proximal diffusion of the frames in the Arab Spring – with activists

engaging with others with whom they identified or who were spatially or culturally

relevant to them (Soule 2004). This diffusion of frames could occur with or without

direct personal contact. When the frames were available through different channels (in

---

[40] Snow et al. (1986) use the term "frame alignment" to cover four framing processes in social movement organisation and mobilisation. They are a) frame bridging, b) frame amplification, c) frame extension and d) frame transformation. In particular, frame bridging and frame amplification describe that ideologically congruent but structurally different frames regarding a particular issue can create linkage and then resonate intra- and inter-groups through interpretation in alignment with the value and belief of the groups. The latter two processes mainly focus on how frames can be extended to other potential activists and groups by adding more meaning or transforming the old meanings into other ones.

this case, through both social media and mass media) and contained some elements in common with other movements, they could be borrowed and copied by other activists (McAdam & Rucht 1993). Hence, similar frames were found in the later Egypt uprising.

When the Tunisians began their uprising, their circumstances and the frames employed, informed, and summoned a large number of supporters in Egypt through social media. For example, the 'Egyptians supporting the Tunisian revolution' Facebook page kept updating its reports of the situation in Tunisia and stimulated discussions among the Egyptians (Rane & Salem 2012). Rane and Salem (2012) believe that the Egyptians were inspired and encouraged by the events in Tunisia. In Egypt, people suffered in similar repressive social, economic, and political conditions under the ruling of Hosni Mubarak's government (Carty 2015), and so shared the same grievances as the Tunisians against their own government (Rane & Salem 2012). When the young Egyptian, 28-year-old Khaled Said, was brutally beaten to death by Egyptian police because he had distributed evidence of police corruption online, the Egyptian uprising was triggered (Frangonikoloppoulos & Chapsos 2012). Following this incident, a Facebook page, 'We are all Khaled Said', was established, in Arabic, by a Google executive, Wael Ghonim (Carty 2015). An English version followed. According to the description on the Facebook page in English, Khaled Said's death was framed as:

> Khaled Said, a 28-year-old Egyptian from the coastal city of

Alexandria, Egypt, was tortured to death at the hands of two police officers. Several eye witnesses described how Khaled was taken by the two policemen into the entrance of a residential building where he was brutally punched and kicked. The two policemen banged his head against the wall, the staircase and the entrance steps. Despite his calls for mercy and asking them why they are doing this to him, they continued their torture until he died according to many eye witnesses. (*About* in 'We are all Khaled Said', viewed 11 August 2018)

The framing in Khaled's story presents some similarities to that of Mohamed Bouazizi's: both stories emphasised that the victims were normal, young, and innocent citizens suffered from unemployment; Khaled and Mohamed should have been protected instead of being tortured and humiliated by the officials in the streets; they were victimised because they revealed the injustice and the corruption of the government; and they both finally died in a dramatic and horrifying way. In comparison with Khaled's innocence and his identity as an ordinary young Egyptian, the violence of the policemen was amplified. This contrast also reflects the corruption of the government. Further, by using 'We are all Khaled Said' as the name of the Facebook page, its creator reminded readers that 'all' of 'us' in Egypt could be the next Khaled Said. Thus, this framing creates a sense of inclusion and of being part of the majority (Pickerill & Krinsky 2012). This frame united the people who recognised themselves as being similar to Khaled Said, and to incited them to fight against torture, poverty, corruption, and unemployment (Carty 2015; Jenkins 2006).

Three years later, in Hong Kong, a similar framing pattern can be found in the

Umbrella Movement. In this movement, people also staged a demonstration for the instituting of a true democracy. Student activists were one of the major rally groups (Lin 2017). Joshua Wong and the members of Scholarism were mostly recognised as being secondary high school students; their image was presented as young, innocent, fearless, and sincere (Wang 2017b). This image would help them to avoid moral judgement and would reduce negative feeling towards them among the public, even though they instigated radical action, such as "reclaim our Civic Square"[41] (Wang 2017b). As they were "students", there would be less possibility that they would be regarded as "performing a political show" in the movement, and this would boost the credibility of their collective voice (Wang 2017b). Joshua further strengthened his student image through an interview: he stated that he was told to attend class and to obey the rules, but that he loved Hong Kong so much and he felt that he needed to stand up for everyone, even though he was just a student. Through this expression of a political vision and the "love" of Hong Kong, from the mouth of a teenager, Joshua not only successfully attracted the attention of his own generation, but also shamed the parent generation, since it was to be expected that this issue would be taken care

---

[41] According to Wang (2017b), the Civic Square refers to the square outside the Hong Kong Central Government Offices. This name was given by Scholarism during the Anti-M&N movement in 2012. Joshua Wong and Scholarism had successfully summoned protesters to occupy the Civic Square in the Anti-M&N movement and finally pushed the Hong Kong government to retreat from the plan of promoting the Moral and National Education in Hong Kong. In the Netflix documentary, *Joshua: Teenage vs. Superpower* (2017), Joshua regarded the success of the movement as a signal that Hong Kong citizens could win the fight against the Chinese Central Government for democracy. Also, the victory of high school students in the social movement deeply impressed the citizens. Then, the Civic Square became a symbol for the citizens that represents the hope of achieving democracy and true freedom in Hong Kong.

of by the adults (*Joshua: Teenager vs. Superpower* 2017).

On the other hand, Joshua framed the Chief Executive, C.Y. Leung, as the accomplice of the Chinese Central Government and the enemy of Hong Kong citizens. As shown in *figure 5*, Joshua Wong shared two pictures on Facebook from the *Dash* Facebook page. The captions for both, in English, read "C.Y. Leung, history will remember what you have done to your people". The posts juxtaposed Leung's photo, taken in the press conference in which he claimed that the movement was illegal, with the photos of the Hong Kong police using violence to disperse the protesting public. With these portraits, Joshua stressed that Leung, instead of listening to his people and protecting them from the decisions of the Chinese Central Government, chose to obey the Central Government and use his well-equipped police force to repress the unarmed public. Thus, the government and Leung were portrayed as the perpetrators of violence.

(Figure 5: The framing puts an equation mark between C.Y. Leung and the police

reactions to the radical public in the movement. Viewed 10 August 2018)

The escalating conflict between the police and the activists also recalled to the public

the impression of the Tiananmen Square Protest in Beijing, in 1989.[42] Some people

wrote on Facebook that they "Feel the same as on the eve of the Tiananmen Square

Protest" (see *figure 6*). This post drew a parallel between the Umbrella Movement and

the Tiananmen Square Protest: the goals of the protests, the major participants, the

oppressors, and the growing tensions were the same. Also, a pessimistic prediction

was implied, with a feeling of fear: like the Tiananmen Square Protest, the conflict in

the Umbrella Movement might end up with a similar massive toll of dead and injured.

---

[42] The Tiananmen Square Protest (also called "六四" or "六四事件", means the 4th June Incident) in 1989 is a prohibited topic in China of which only some blurry data and vague evidence can be found in domestic research. Based on Flynn and Hutcheson's memoirs (2015), the protest was initially an assembly by university students, intellectuals, factory workers and city residents to mourn the death of Yaobang HU, who was a liberal reformer and also the former General Secretary of the Chinese Communist Party. Later, the rally evolved into a huge movement to claim greater democracy and transparency in governance. The students at Tiananmen Square started a hunger strike to call the government's attention and quickly motivated people in more than 150 cities to join the protest (Majerol & Perlman 2014). The government outlawed the protest and used military force to repress the rally at Tiananmen Square on the 4th of June 1989. Due to the number of dead and injured (exact numbers remain unknown) during the conflict, some Western media also called the repression of 4th June as the Tiananmen Square massacre (Flynn & Hutcheson 2015).

(Figure 6: A post describing the feeling of the Umbrella Movement was "the same as

on the eve of the Tiananmen Square Protest". Viewed 30 July 2018)

The Scholarism Facebook page also shared a photo of a wounded middle school

student in uniform (*figure 7*) and commented: "They dare to beat a student?" Through

this framing, this post seemed to attribute the student's wounds to the policemen

surrounding him, and implied that they were the perpetrators. Thus, the conflict

between the police and the public was further amplified.

(Figure 7: A middle school student in uniform with bleeding lips was surrounded by

the police. Viewed 13 August 2018)

The framing tactics employed in the Umbrella Movement were similar to those of the

Arab Spring. First, the movements had common goals and values: freedom, justice,

political rights, and ultimately democracy. Second, they all tried to frame their

governments and officials as representing violence and as enemies of the people: Ben

Ali's regime and Fedia Hamdi in Tunisia; Hosni Mubarak's regime and the police in

Egypt; the Chinese Central Government, C.Y. Leung, and the police in Hong Kong. Third, innocent, non-violent victims were harmed by the forces during the uprisings, who then became symbols of the movements: Mohamed Bouazizi was insulted by Fedia Hamdi, and sacrificed himself to awaken in the public an awareness of their lack of freedom; Khaled Said was killed by the police because he revealed the corruption of the countries; Joshua Wong was arrested during the strike because he fought against the superpower of the Chinese government. Framing the stories from the activists' viewpoint triggered the protests, and the momentum of the movements was maintained because the frames successfully presented the validity of their claims, provoking outrage and resonating with an already aggrieved public (Snow et al. 1986). Through Facebook, these frames successfully virtualised the offline issues and brought them into debates online, to be widely disseminated. By this point, the pattern of virtualising the actual dimension in augmented revolutions has been proved.

However, a critical question arises in connection with this framing: to what extent did these stories reflect the truth? Lim (2013) reveals that Ali Bouazizi has told "white lies" in his post about Mohamed Bouazizi's death. Actually, Mohamed was just an ordinary poor young man who never finished high school. Moreover, no one could prove that Fedia Hamdi had, in fact, slapped Mohamed; this was a story added by Ali, without any strong evidence. During Lim's research (2013), Fedia Hamdi repeatedly assured that she had never hit Mohamed Bouazizi. Ali skilfully used framing to guide the online audiences and increase their awareness of the brutality of the government.

With the inclusion of these two fabrications in his story, the death of Mohamed

Bouazizi became motivational (Lim 2013), and the tide of public opinion in the

country turned against the ruling regime. This evidence indicates that virtualising the

actual world through social media is not equal to duplicating scenes from the actual

world.

The same logic applies when the activists use framing in the description of a photo.

For example, the picture shown in *figure 7* did not reveal how the student in Hong

Kong got hurt or who was responsible. Another possible interpretation is that the

police surrounded the wounded student in order to protect him from the protesting

crowd; it is possible that he was hurt by the protesters themselves in the chaos of the

demonstration. The student's facial expression did not show any emotion of hatred

toward the police surrounding him; and the police did not catch or hold the student as

if arresting a criminal – which was, at least, much better than in Joshua Wong's

scenario.[43] The only explicit intention apparent in the picture is that the police wanted

to separate the student from the crowd. It would be reasonable to write: "Policemen

rescued a student who was hurt in the radical action of a protesting site". While the

former interpretation attributes blame to the police and aims to incite outrage against

them and the government, the latter interpretation seems to praise the reliability of the

---

[43] In the documentary, *Joshua: Teenage vs. Superpower* (2017), there is a scene where Joshua
Wong is knocked around by the policemen and he is removed from the Civic Square to a patrol
wagon.

Hong Kong police, while blaming the aggressive protesters.

So, it is crucial to note that the use framing to frame a scenario is a double-edged sword for the activists. The authorities who want to suppress the movement can apply the same method. In telling a story from a particular perspective, social media framing can determine the direction of the public opinion regarding a social movement. This is explicitly different from traditional movements in which mass media dominated the framing process.

'We are all Khaled Said'

Using social media, marginalised groups, which were excluded in the actual world, now can join the debate on public issues, easily and equally (Asen 2000; Bennett 2012; Castells 2012; Loader & Mercea 2011; Warner 2002); also, social media enables users to actively seek and network with other like-minded people online and make their voices heard instantly (Castells 2012; Lee et al. 2015). This trend can now be observed through the active use of Facebook pages as online communities, to share information and discuss issues.

During the Egyptian uprising, 'We are all Khaled Said' was the activists' most popular Facebook pages, helping them to network worldwide. To the date of writing, this page had received 287,454 'likes' and had been 'followed' by 281,018 people (see *figure 8*). The Facebook pages of Scholarism and of Joshua Wong are similarly popular, and have been 'liked' and 'followed' by over 300,000 users (see also *figure 8*). In van Dijck's opinion (2013), a large number of 'likes' and followers will boost the popularity of a post, attracting additional audiences and subsequently, members to the online communities responsible for uploading it; any comment shared on these pages may well be seen by very many like-minded people. This is not normally achievable in the actual dimension, without social media.

(Figure 8: Screenshots of the Facebook pages of We Are All Khaled Said, Scholarism

and Joshua Wong. Viewed 14 August 2018)

Boyd (2010) reminds us that in such online communities, the "networked public", a

horizontally structured interpersonal network reliant on the social media connection

between individuals, is gradually realised. Even though people in those communities

were invisible to each other, they could stay together if they were the "same" under a

certain frame (Snow et al. 1986). In the Egyptian uprising, the activists saw

themselves as the "next" Khaled Said, facing threats from the government; the Hong

Kong protesters styled themselves as "Hongkongers", demanding the return of their

stolen democracy (Lin 2017). Scholars (Laclau 2005; McGarty et al. 2014) maintain

that even though the demands of each individual in the actual world are unique, by

framing a common opposition to the status quo or the ruling power, a "popular

identity" may be built in a Facebook community, which will then standardise the

demands of its members. People from different backgrounds can thus be united in

social movements and fight for a common goal.

While Gladwell (2010) argues that interpersonal relationships on social media are

mostly built between acquaintances and are usually very weak, Jurgenson (2012)

asserts that the friendships built in the actual world also exist in the virtual world.

This latter argument suggests the possibility that individuals could be influenced by

the revolutionary frames on, for example, Facebook, networked into an online

activism community and connected to social movements directly through their friends

online. Research also shows that Facebook users who have more offline contacts are

more civically engaged (Jurgenson 2011). To demonstrate, in the screenshot of the

Scholarism page shown in *figure 8*, there is a line indicating that, in total, five friends liked or checked-in to that page. This implies that those friends are at least supporters of Scholarism – even if they did not interact digitally with members or protest in person – and that their posts would be more encouraging to their friends in the actual world.

Moreover, social media has a mechanism to allow users to stay connected with their networks. For instance, when Facebook is set to its default setting, any interactive action by a user – clicking the 'like' button, updating a status, sharing a post, tagging someone, or being tagged (for example, as shown in *figure 1*, some users were tagged as being with the sender of the post during the protest at Tahrir Square) – will send a notification to the user's networks (see *figure 9*). Awareness of a social movement can be increased among activists' networks through such notifications. Lim (2017) sees individual activists as the "nodes" in the "rhizomatic assemblages" which horizontally connect different assemblages online. Revolutionary messages can be further disseminated across assemblages according to the proximal diffusion model, and through frame bridging and frame amplification (Soule 2004; Snow et al. 1986). Therefore, the Arab Spring and the Umbrella Movement were not only local movements taking place 'in the flesh', but became international movements supported globally by a wide range of online participants.

Above all, current social movements are being virtualised with mediation and framing through social media. When movements extend to the virtual world, they can be

participated in and spread widely through networked publics and rhizomatic

assemblages. Also, people who networked together are reminded to stay in contact

with their friends on social media. Thus, their physical lives are increasingly merged

with their virtual lives.

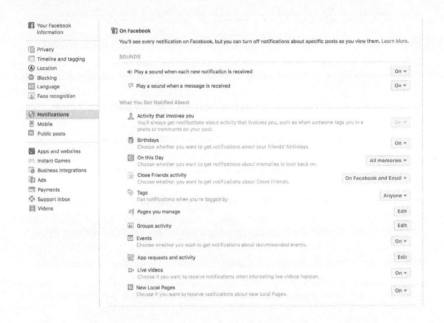

(Figure 9: Setting page on Facebook. Viewed 15 August 2018)

Chapter 3 Actualising the Virtual World

In this chapter, I will focus on the alternative direction of information flow, as suggested in my argument apropos of augmented revolution: the actualisation of the protests and networks from the virtual world to the actual world. Some recent studies have asserted that digital activities can lead to offline protest actions (Burean & Badescu 2014; Lee & Chan 2018). In addition, Huat (2017, p. 122) points out that "the Umbrella Movement can be placed not only in the lineage of Occupy Wall Street but also that of the momentous Arab Spring Uprising". By suggesting that these movements are similar, the scholar firstly points out that occupying a physical space with social media use is a common trend in contemporary movements. Second, he implies that social movements may travel from one region to the next – indeed, this could be observed when the Tunisian uprising triggered the Egyptian uprising through social media in the Arab Spring. This chapter, therefore, argues that as social media gradually make for an augmented reality, online actions – such as the social media activity during the Arab Spring and the Umbrella Movement – can and do have an effect on offline protests.

Mobilising through posting

Activists and their global audiences relied heavily on social media for interaction during the Arab Spring and the Umbrella Movement. By responding to the posts, the audiences were already participating digitally in the movements. Jurgenson (2012)

argues that a person may have a (real life) close friend who is participating in protests

and staying in direct contact via social media at the same time, in which case, that

person is more likely to be influenced by his or her close friend's opinions and be

encouraged to participate in high-risk actions, due to the interpersonal trust (Benson

& Rochon 2004; Brym et al. 2014). According to this logic, the friendship mediated

online increases the influences of the content shared on social media. Also, networked

celebrities on social media are likely to be able to mobilise the public, since they may

speak with authority regarding certain relevant information and can directly interact

with audiences (Tufekci 2013). Recent evidence indicates that sharing social

movement related content on social media has a strong impact on the physical actions

carried out in social movements (Frangonikoloppoulos & Chapsos 2012; Huat 2017;

Lee et al. 2017). The above arguments lead the discussion to the question: what is the

impact of social media content, and how do the materials in the virtual dimension

mobilise offline participation?

From my textual analysis of the Facebook posts of 'We are all Khaled Said' and

Scholarism during the Arab Spring and the Umbrella Movement, I discern two main

categories, classified according to content: information based and affect based. The

information based posts aim to provide useful information for audiences about the

ongoing protests; the affect based posts aim to evoke specific emotions, such as

outrage, frustration, and resentment, among audiences and mobilise them to act.

The information based posts can be divided into two sub-types. Posts of the first type provides plain information about the facts of the movement and contains a little of the framing element. *Figure 1* shows a good example of the information oriented posts during the Egyptian uprising. Similarly, the post shown in *figure 10* only explained the reason for the gathering of the crowd. These plain information posts catch the attention of the audiences and may lead to some basic following actions such as 'liking', reposting, or commenting. However, it is difficult to be sure that these posts would lead to further radical action in the actual protests.

(Figure 10: An information based post explains what is happening in the photo.

Viewed 9 August 2018)

The second type of information based posts provide strategies and suggestions for activists, in order to facilitate the actual protests. For instance, during the Umbrella Movement, Scholarism released a guide to one of the occupying protests, 'One tent per person' (see *figure 11*). The post gave information on the location of Scholarism's tent, the activities on the site, the location and opening time of the public bathrooms, and a list of items suggested for the protest and their recommended price range. Compared with the first type, the messages delivered in this post were more practical and supportive of the protests. The post does not contain any language that appeals to the emotions, either; rather, it becomes an ancillary guide to implementing strategies for occupying a physical space. Consequently, this post is more likely to be shared among protesters and its advice adopted when occupying the streets.

(Figure 11: A guide to the protest of "One tent per person". Viewed 13 August 2018)

Affect based posts are intended to incite audiences to act by evoking specific emotions through shocking, especially visual, materials, with well thought out motivational language and a clear call to action. These expressions could be linked to the process of framing. In intentionally adding their own interpretation and opinions to a fragment of fact, the activists point out what they see as the most urgent problems to solve, and who is the enemy; they make their audiences mindful of violations of their beliefs, arousing negative emotions (see e.g. *figure 6*).

There is also profound power in images. I do, indeed, feel anxious, worried, sad, terrified, angry, or upset when I look at some of the images relevant to the protests (for example, the photos of Khaled Said before and after he was beaten by the police[44]; also, see *figure 12*). Visual elements can evoke and intensify grievances among the audiences. The amplified grievances will give attitudinal support to the movement, and resonating with onlookers or sympathisers through social media, and finally engaging them in the protests through a call for action (Lee et al. 2017). This viewpoint is supported by Castells (2012), who regards social media as a network of outrage and hope, which, through sharing relevant information, can inflame the outrage of the citizens and encourage them to act in protest. Similarly, Tang (2015) suggests that "war-like" images of the protests, shared through television and social media, will stimulate "instant grievances" among audience members and motivate

---

[44] See http://www.elshaheeed.co.uk/home-khaled-said-full-story-background-truth-what-happened-torture-in-egypt-by-egyptian-police/.

them to act. He states that at the beginning of the Umbrella Movement, Hong Kong

society did not expect the use of tear gas; this "suddenly imposed" radical method,

used by the police to scatter the protesters, horrified the public, and grievances against

the police became the reason for participation by the protesters mobilised by these

images. Such grievances were "instant" through the mediation of visual images

shared through television and social media; they could not otherwise have swelled to

such magnitude in such a short time. Potts (2015) also notes that photography played

a crucial role in promoting resistance to an oppressive government. In the Tunisian

uprising, photos distributed on social media not only documented the atrocities of a

violent state response, but also revealed the political upheaval around the region to the

world.

Other research suggests that the increasing power of imagery to mobilise is due to a

cultural preference for the use of visual images on social media (Lee & Ting 2015).

According to the findings, Scholarism's Facebook page delivered huge numbers of

'lazybones picture packages'[45] to attract the attention of the young and convince them

to repost. In short, Scholarism skilfully used both framing and images to construct and

spread its statements about the Umbrella Movement and, at the same time, what it

shared online keeps guiding and encouraging its audiences to respond and to act

---

[45] A lazybones picture package refers to a picture with a brief explanation. The package usually contains ironic and humorous ideas that easily attract youngsters' attention and encourage them to repost without the need of extra editing (Lee & Ting 2015).

through social media, or with their bodies on streets.

(Figure 12: The "line of defence" on Nathan Road, near Mong Kok, one of the

occupied sites during the Umbrella Movement. Protesters used stark fence and bins to

build a border, and used umbrellas and simple self-made weapons to protect the

protest site from the police's evacuation. Viewed 13 August 2018.)

The evidence cited above indicates that the framing in the posts and the visual

materials archived on social media will significantly affect its audiences' decision

regarding joining social movements. Yet, it is important to note that the content posted

on social media does not necessarily cause similar effects at the individual level (Tang

2015). The shocking posts may have frightened and discouraged some citizens from

joining the movements. In both the Arab Spring and the Umbrella Movement, the

most overt and direct conflicts mediated on social media were between the unarmed

protesters and the well-equipped police forces. The violent conflict and the shocking images of it may well have led to the retreat of potential activists. Also, mediated "instant grievances" are not the only factor that mobilises the public to join movements; they may also be encouraged by the political goals and hopes embedded in the movements – for example, dignity, freedom, democracy in the Arab Spring (see *figure 13*), and genuine suffrage in the Umbrella Movement.

However, Papacharissi and Trevey (2018) argue that protest actions in the era of social media are less politically based and less oriented towards collective goals under the horizontal and relatively loose structure of networked publics. It is an impossible requirement that all of the participants of a social movement should share a collective political background and knowledge and unite under a clear political goal, especially when the social movements are mediated to the virtual sphere as fragments and spread internationally. Rather, participants are mobilised by various, and perhaps personal, motivations, and united in small groups based on other considerations, or they may even act at an individual level (Anduiza et al. 2014; Bennett & Segerberg 2013; Lee et al.2017). In line with the notion of the affective public (Paracharissi 2014), this thesis asserts that, compared with complex political statements, the mediated "instant grievance" is a more straightforward, common, and direct emotional factor to resonate with people and trigger online and offline protest actions on a global scale.

We are all Khaled Said
29 January 2011 ·

I never tasted Freedom & Democracy before in my whole life. Most young protesters out on the streets never did. One day, very soon I hope, we will. Your support is vital to bring this day forward. Plz consider joining a protest near you to support Egyptians uprizing. There are protests almost in every single country in the world.

I'll leave you enjoy this video. Can't stop watching it. Can we have more of these plz?

GDATA.YOUTUBE.COM
Egyptian Revolution Jan 25th 2011 - Take what's Yours!
Credits to Tamer Shaaban who made this video important message to...

230   57 Comments

(Figure 13: A post asks the audiences to support the Egyptian uprising for chasing

freedom and democracy. Viewed 9 August 2018.)

Connective actions and communal spaces

According to Papacharissi and Trevey's insights regarding social media networks

(2018) and Bennett and Segerberg's logic of connective actions (2013), networked

publics are not subjected to strong organisational control; individuals are permitted to

express interest in or allegiance to issues "without having to enter the complex

negotiation of personal vs. collective politics" (Papacharissi & Trevey 2018, p. 91).

Thus, connective actions can be developed out of personalised reactions to

movements, based on the social media connection. This section will focus on what

connective actions were mobilised in the Arad Spring and the Umbrella Movement and what they meant to the 'augmented revolution'.

Snow et al. (1986) note that using framing will also allow an issue to extends to a broader theme or be replaced by other meanings in order to resonate with other potential individuals and groups. Thus, various interpretation and frames will appear on social media during social movements, and may mobilise different digital activities in different people, consequently leading to a range of actions offline. In other words, a social movement can be viewed as a mission to be completed by society as a whole, but through different motivations, goals, methods, and paths. Lee et al. (2017) demonstrate that the meaning of participation in a social movement is diverse across participants. They highlight that collective actions following a political goal are still the major part of a movement; however, collective actions are gradually diminished by the emergence of personalised and small-group actions which are affected by interaction on social media and which accompany various personal demands.

The first aspect of connective actions observed in social movements is that synchronous protest actions occur in various regions, domestically and internationally. In the Arab Spring, through social media use, while the death of Mohamed Bouazizi triggered protests in different regions of Tunisia against the ruling regime, the uprising also quickly echoed in Egypt (Carty 2015). According to Rane and Salem's research (2012), a Facebook page called "Egyptians supporting the Tunisian revolution" was created to demonstrate support;[46] the Egyptians shared the same grievances against their own government as the Tunisians, and reports of the Tunisian uprising quickly resonated with them. Later, when the tragedy of Khaled Said occurred and was mediated to social media, the Facebook page 'We are all Khaled Said' was set up, and the Egyptian uprising was instantly ignited across the whole country. Scholars (Carty 2015; Frangonikolopoulos & Chapsos 2012; Rane & Salem 2012) note that not only the Facebook pages, but also the '#' (hashtag) function on Twitter helped to organise connective actions during the Egyptian uprising; in particular, they highlight the hashtag '#Jan25', which represents 25 January 2011, the "Day of Anger", the date of the start of the Egyptian uprising (Frangonikolopoulos & Chapsos 2012). All of the posts on Twitter with the hashtag '#Jan25' added could be linked together and searched and shown at once. Thus, the activists could quickly share the protest relevant information and strategies with each other and attract other Twitter users to join the protests, either online or offline. Up till the date Mubarak was deposed, almost two million tweets were contributed to this hashtag topic (Rane & Salem 2012). Through social media, the activists in Egypt were connected not only the entire Arab world, but also to the far reaches of other continents.

The information based post in *figure 14* indicated that a protest of 3,000 people supporting the Egyptian uprising had been staged in London five days after the

---

[46] Due to the change of use conditions and the policy of Facebook usage, this Facebook page no longer exist at the date of writing this thesis.

uprising broke out. This could be recognised as evidence of the global connective

actions facilitated by social media.

(Figure 14: A protest also happened in London to support the Egyptian uprising.

Viewed 9 August 2018)

During the Umbrella Movement, the protests in Hong Kong also inspired some

personalised actions around the world in support of the local protesters. For instance,

Scholarism reposted an article from *Dash* (*figure 15*) demonstrating support from

foreign students who recognised themselves as members of the Umbrella Movements.

In the Netherlands, some activists also posted flyers with the slogan 'I want genuine

suffrage' under the road sign for Hongkongstraat in Amsterdam, to promote the

movement underway in Hong Kong. The flyer, in black and white, also used the word

'撐 ('cheng', meaning 'to support' or 'to hold' in Chinese; 'Steun' in Dutch) with the symbol of an umbrella to represent, simultaneously, 'hold your umbrella' and 'support the Umbrella Movement'. During the movement, a big screen was installed in Admiralty, Hong Kong, called 'Add Oil Machine' ('加油机, meaning a machine of encouragement) to collect and display supportive messages on social media from all over the world, in order to encourage the local protesters (Lee & Chan 2018). So, even if activists could not physically attend the protests on the main street in Hong Kong, they could still connect and contribute to the Umbrella Movement by using social media. Through their actions around the world, activists abroad could attract local attention to the movements. Thus personalised and small-group protest actions in different regions can be mediated by social media, sent to the networks of the protesters and so reinforce the momentum of the local protest.

(Figure 15: Examples of personalised and small-group actions around the world to

support the Umbrella Movement. Viewed 13 August 2018)

Other typical online connective actions during the Umbrella Movement can be

observed. First the activists encouraged their friends through social media to sign the

digital petitions on the White House's office website requesting the U.S. government

to "press the Chinese government to honour its promise of democratic elections to the

Hong Kong citizenry." (Griffiths 2014; Lin 2017; see also *figure 16*[47]). According to

the news (Griffiths 2014), a petition received around 200,000 signatures from

supporters around the world and, in response, the White House spokesman showed a

positive attitude towards the petition.

---

[47] The original link to the petition no longer exists.

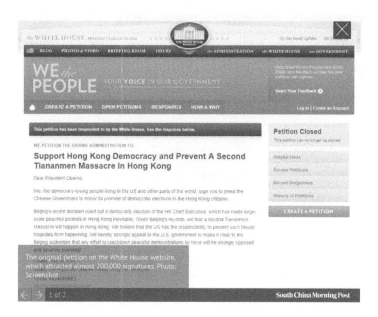

(Figure 16: The petition launched on the White House website during the Umbrella

Movement. Viewed 28 August 2018.)

Meanwhile, users on Facebook began a spontaneous campaign to change their

Facebook profile pictures to an image of a yellow ribbon on a black background (see

figure 17), thus signalling their concurrence and demonstrating their support for the

Umbrella Movement. On the other hand, the opponents of the movement changed

their Facebook profile pictures to an image of a blue ribbon (Lee & Chan 2018). In

fact, changing the Facebook profile pictures as part of a campaign is not a rare

phenomenon today. After the Paris terror attack in 2015, numerous Facebook users

also changed their profile pictures to mourn the people who died in that incident.

Morozov (2011a) may categorise these campaigns under his term 'slacktivism';

however, Lin (2017) believes that the profile picture, as a social media meme, should

be taken seriously in the movement when it became a prevalent symbol. Nissenbaum

and Shifman (2015) point out that the pervasive mimicry of the profile picture is a

mechanism that underpins the construction of "sameness" in the decentralised context

of online space. Yet, this thesis argues that 'sameness' is not necessarily equal to

'collective' in a broad sense. According to Bennett and Segerberg's logic (2013;

Papacharissi & Trevey 2018), it is difficult to assert that there is a united goal and/or

understanding of the movement behind the massive adoption of the image of the

yellow ribbon. Also, it is unwise to claim that the people who did not change their

profile pictures did not support the movement. In this sense, changing the profile

pictures is only one of the effective ways to allocate individuals to an online

community.

Interestingly, Lin (2017) mentions that social media memes even provoked a spate of

'unfriending' during the movement – in which, simultaneously on Facebook and in

the actual world, people 'unfriended' a friend who held a different political opinion.

Although the exact number of the cases of unfriending in the actual domain is not

large according to a data analysis, statements and debates on social media about social

issues will affect users' behaviours in both the virtual and actual domains (Lee &

Chan 2018).[48]

(Figure 17: Examples of the yellow ribbon profile picture in the Umbrella Movement.

Viewed 31 July 2018.)

In both the Arab Spring and the Umbrella Movement, interactions on social media were finally actualised in the other dimension, as the physical occupation of real spaces. This is also one of the outstanding shared hallmarks of both movements. This is a result of the transformation of time and space in the digital era: "(m)obile networked communication fosters a form of virtual time and space, which is superimposed onto territorial space" (Potts 2015, p. 51). Through social media, activists could immerse in their virtual networks while sitting in physical spaces. In

---

[48] Lee and Chan (2018) conducted a survey on the activists' behaviour in social media during the Umbrella Movement. 969 activists in Admiralty participated in the survey in October. 17.1% of them had actually unfriended people. Another 273 and 296 activists in Admiralty and Mong Kok were studied in November. 25% and 35% of them had unfriended actual friends, respectively.

this process, they could bring their online friends to the physical present and gave new meanings to urban spaces, and then made the occupation of these spaces symbolic for their movements (AlSayyad & Guvenc 2015; Hui 2017).

Scholars agree that in both movements, the places chosen to stage the protests have their own historical backgrounds and practical meanings. Bourguiba Avenue in Tunisia,[49] Tahrir Square in Egypt,[50] 'Civic Square' and Central in Hong Kong[51] are the arterial roads and symbolic places critical to daily business and governance (AlSayyad 2011; Hui 2017). By physically occupying and so paralysing the functions of these spaces, the protesters first demonstrated a threat to the political authorities (Jurgenson 2012), then, through their takeover and occupation, the spaces acquired new meanings (AlSayyad & Guvenc 2015; Hui 2017). In Egypt, during the protest, clinics, kindergartens, tents, media centres, and even concerts and other rituals

---

[49] According to AlSayyad & Guvenc (2015), Bourguiba Avenue was one of the major protest hubs in the Tunisian uprising. It was named after Habib Bourguiba, the previous ruler of Egypt who was ousted by Ben Ali in 1987. This avenue can be accessed through numerous other streets and thus it is difficult for the security forces to block in the protest. The Interior Ministry and the French embassy are also located along this avenue. The authors believe that there is an ironic meaning to the protesters' choosing to rally there to overthrow Ben Ali's regime.

[50] According to AlSayyad & Guvenc (2015), Tahrir Square is located in the centre of modern Cairo, which is surrounded by many important buildings, like the Egyptian Museum, the Mugamma, and the headquarter of the Arab League. Like the Bourguiba Avenue, the Square is constituted of five to six adjoining spaces, combing intersections of more than ten streets and two bridges. Therefore, it is difficult for the government to secure. This was where the 1952 revolution happened to end the governance of a king and turn Egypt into a republic. Tahrir also means "liberty" in the local language.

[51] Central is the major commercial district in Hong Kong where big banks and international corporations (for example, Bank of China, HSBC), famous sightseeing points (for example, Lan Kwai Fong), large shopping malls (for example, SoHo), and the hub of the government are located.

emerged in Tahrir Square. Similarly, in Hong Kong, as well as normal functional

tents, various creative functional areas for facilitating the occupiers' daily lives were

built at the sites of occupation. For example: the occupiers of Harcourt Road,

Admiralty, renamed the road 'Harcourt Village' (Hui 2017) and set up a 'big stage' for

disseminating news, as a platform for speeches delivered by key activists, and for

sharing opinions among the participants; self-study areas (see e.g. *figure 18*) were

built for the students to study while engaged in the sit-in in the village; the 'Lennon-

wall' (see also *figure 18*) was built for visitors to leave their messages of

encouragement and hope for Hong Kong (Hui 2017).

(Figure 18: One of the self-study areas in Admiralty and the Lennon-Wall. Viewed 29

August 2018.)

At the same time, people who actively took part in the protests were taking care of

each other (Lin 2017). In some occupied areas, makeshift supply stations were set up

by citizens and volunteers to provide free food, water, and other necessities to support

the protesters (Hui 2017). In order to solve the problem of toilets on the protest sites

for female protesters, some protesters sought help from the public, and Scholarism

also helped them to spread the messages on Facebook (see *figure 19*). According to

the comments displayed, citizens were willing to help, including by donation, by

asking their friends who work as designer or even by sharing their private property

with the public.

(Figure 19: A post showing protesters tried to solve the toilet problem for female

protesters. Viewed 13 August 2018.)

By reproducing (as much as possible) their everyday lives of online communities in

the protests, by turning the online communities into villages in the occupied sites and

by showing care for each other, the protestors created a new form of social life during

the course of the social movements (Halvorsen 2015). In the case of the Umbrella

Movement, the "villagers" in different villages set different goals and courses for their

actions, but all came within the concept of a "caring society" (Lim 2017).

Additionally, humorous names were given to the tents in the occupied areas, art

exhibits and performances were staged (see *figure 20*), and songs were written in

support of the movement (Lee & Chan 2018) – for example, *Upholding the Umbrella*,

the movement's unofficial 'anthem' by Denise Ho and others, and *Jia Ming* by Kay

Tse in 2014.[52] By adding these creative, playful but also caring elements to the protest

actions, the sense of community was foregrounded (Hui 2017). Thus the political

orientation of the social movement was diminished, or at least pushed into the

background, while the carnival-like features were highlighted by social media; the

protests were no longer purely political, rather, they could be seen as community-

oriented. In this way, new understandings are given to the connective actions in

contemporary social movements.

[52] Unlike *Upholding the Umbrella*, *Jia Ming* does not directly speak for the Umbrella Movement. However, the lyrics are interpreted as alluding and worshiping the efforts of the protesters. This song was quickly adopted by the supporters of the movement after its release. The music video of *Jia Ming* produced by the protesters is available on YouTube <https://www.youtube.com/watch?v=tbZpNo_xP3c >. Kay Tse's album, *Kontinue*, which contains this song, cannot be searched and downloaded in the Mainland China due to its association with the Umbrella Movement.

(Figure 20: A playful name, "No.3 Royal Admiralty", was given to a tent in the "Harcourt Village"; the statue of the 'Umbrella Man'; and a dance performance on the occupied site. Viewed 29 August 2018.)

Hui (2017) also points out that new utopian communities are emerging from occupied sites. During contemporary social movements, streets and squares no longer serve their original purpose. Instead, they are communal places overlaid by the virtual network sphere, in which activists can continue their fight, along with their efforts online, and live with their friends whom they met in online communities. In other words, the protesters' online interpersonal relationships have been realised in the actual dimension in a form of community; what Gladwell (2010) sees as "weak ties" online have become stronger and closer with face-to-face interaction in the actual world and significantly enhance the level of participation (Pickerill & Krinsky 2012). The social movements thus evolve into 'augmented revolution'.

Who speaks for whom?

Boyd (2010), Castells (2012), Bennett and Segerberg (2013), and Lim (2017) have stressed that contemporary social media facilitated social movements are working under a decentralised, horizontal, rhizomatically connected structure, but whether those movements have become leaderless is still controversial. Shirky (2008) remarks, however, that the use of social media has broken the hierarchical structure headed by powerful persons or groups, allowing for organising without organisations. Participants in the Occupy Wall Street movement and the Egyptian uprising asserted that they were leaded by no one, but Gerbaudo (2012) finds this idea suspect, arguing that the leaders on social media can be invisible, but that the logic of communication in the hierarchical structure still remains. Although any social media users can express themselves online, most of the influential communication flow on social media today is still controlled by a handful of people, who effectively frame the protests, directing people's attention and inflaming the participants' emotions. There is evidence of this in the finding of Wilson and Dunn's investigation into 106,563 tweets which employed the #Jan25 hashtag during the Egyptian uprising (2011). They discovered that the great majority of messages were sent by 200 influential accounts, which demonstrates that, on Twitter, a minority of users produced the content for consumption by the majority.

Gerbaudo (2012) argues further, that when an influential Facebook administrator or a celebrity on Tweeter updates a status or talks about an incident involving the police, they are not only "informing", but "inviting a certain kind of emotional response" or "physical reaction" from the audiences (p. 139). Although they are not giving orders, they are indeed, through calculated and emotive language, mobilising their audiences to act (Papacharissi & Trevey 2018). It is therefore unwise to consider current social movements as absolutely spontaneous and leaderless.

If we use van Dijck's principle of popularity (2013) to analyse the terms 'influential' and 'celebrity' as used in the digital sphere, we find that someone could be influential or famous online if his or her opinions receive a large enough number of "likes", or comments, or reposting. From this perspective, this thesis argues that there may well be no fixed leaders on social media, because anyone and everyone could potentially be an opinion leader. It is interesting to note here the contradiction that while social media seems to reallocate the power of communication in the interpersonal relationships online, it also gives rise to a new form of leadership in a more competitive and chaotic environment.

To avoid an overlap with the leadership existing in the actual domain, Gerbaudo suggests the notion of "soft leaders" for the leaders of contemporary social media facilitated social movements (2012). This leadership is built upon the participatory character of web 2.0, in a dialogical or interactive form. The leaders are normally not visible; in the early stages of the movements, they do not perceive themselves as leaders, and even refuse to be so labelled. However, they do, in fact, set scripts and scenes, and prepare emotional arguments to diffuse through their networks. Regarding the Arab Spring, Gerbaudo (2012) recognises the creator of the Facebook page 'We are all Khaled Said', Wael Ghonim, as the soft leader of the Egyptian uprising; Lin (2017) suggests that Joshua Wong was the soft leader of the Umbrella Movement. Although Joshua refused to be labelled a leader, he admitted that someone should stand as a symbol of the movement. He finally recognised himself as the convenor of the protests and that he should take responsibility for the safety of the protesters, as well as for breaking the law (*Joshua: Teenager vs. Superpower* 2017). The 'soft leader' may indeed be the case, since a social movement has at least one and perhaps multiple goals to achieve, and the element of collective actions still remains; it is therefore important to have someone to maintain the enthusiasm of the protesters and guide the organisational practices in the actual world.

The traditional collective leadership shrank and became "soft" due to decentralised networks on social media. This means that even famous leaders can no longer unify public opinion and represent all groups collectively. This problem of the soft leadership sustains in the actual protests. When the online group members were encouraged to join the protests with various reasons, it was difficult to allocate one leader to guide or speak for all of them. Ling (2004) argues that in order to gain direct access to protest relevant information and communication online one needs to be Internet savvy, and Internet literacy may well isolate the movement leaders from those less Internet savvy. The gulf between the new soft leadership and old-fashioned audiences may generate conflicts concerning the values, protest approaches and intentions of a movement. Bennett ad Segerberg (2013) subsequently point out that connective actions in contemporary social movements count on the informal conversation of personalised frames within the social networks, without forming a massive alignment on one specific political idea. So it is highly possible that different assemblages could take a stance towards the protests and the movement that differed from the collective one. If the soft leaders were to try to speak for these groups, this could lead to resistance from the assemblages and trigger an organisational crisis in the movement.

Lin (2017) mentions such a conflict: some representatives of the student leaders of the Umbrella Movement had come to Mong Kok, one of the occupied areas, to communicate with the public there in order to add the occupiers' appeals to their own claims. This action triggered outrage among the occupiers and ended up as a dispute, with the occupiers shouting, "You cannot represent me". Similar cases occurred

widely, across various occupied areas, implying that the student leaders could not

effectively organise the crowd (Lin 2017). Although some scholars interviewed in the

documentary *Joshua: Teenager vs. Superpower* (2017) believe that Scholarism had

successfully hijacked the Occupy Central with Love and Peace (OCLP) and turned it

into a big social movement, the leaders of Scholarism had to concede that they lost

control of the movement as a whole. As time passed, the actions of the protesters

gradually became contrary to the leaders' plans and expectations (*Joshua: Teenager

vs. Superpower* 2017). Thus, in the Umbrella Movement, the students, as soft leaders,

could not regulate but could only advocate what the activists should do; their

leadership and representation in the actual world were diminished and restrained by

the horizontal structure that was constituted online and strengthened through social

media. While Gerbaudo (2012) and Lin (2017) believe that soft leadership is still

central to mobilisation in contemporary social movements, connective actions

facilitated by social media add more uncertainties to the sustainability and the

eventual destination of the movements.

Conclusion

The use of social media in contemporary social movements is increasing. This thesis concentrates on the relationship between social media and its users, and asserts that social media enhances the users' abilities in relation to the dynamics of organisation, mobilisation, and contagion in and between the current social movements. This is because social media has become a 'bridge' to extend the actual dimension to the virtual dimension and has 'augmented' our reality. By reallocating access to information and freedom of expression, social media facilitates the emergence of a decentralised structure for social movements. While the protests are virtualised to the digital dimension, what is important online is actualised in the physical world. Thus, through social media use, contemporary social movements have evolved into 'augmented revolutions'. This idea provides a new perspective for understanding the role of social media in contemporary social movements.

In particular, to investigate the role of social media in contemporary social movements, this thesis conducts a comparative analysis of two typical movements: the Arab Spring and the Hong Kong Umbrella Movement. These movements were completely different in terms of goals, cultural background, ICTs infrastructure, political system, and economic developments, but both protests featured the extensive and intense involvement of social media. A clear trend could be observed, in that these movements were no longer restricted to the domestic arena, but, with the reinforcement of social media, became global events (Huat 2017; Lee 2015b; Rane & Salem 2012).

Through the case study, this thesis finds that social media facilitates and accelerates the traditional protest procedure, in terms of mediating, framing, and sharing of information, empowering individual voices, building and connecting online communities, and enhancing interpersonal bonds both online and offline. This thesis asserts that social movements in the actual world are extending to the virtual world through the posts of activists. It is important to note that activists' framing of social media contents is based on their cognition, attitudes, and positions; thus, the posts are not necessarily equal to the public opinion and the objective facts of a situation. However, when their voices were accepted and shared by online communities, those ideas may point a new direction of public opinion for social movements. At the same time, when the movements were mediated, the informal contents on Facebook gradually become an alternative source of protest-related information. This trend emerges when audiences cannot directly access reliable news from mass media, such as television and newspapers. Facebook thus provides a direct link between the protesters and the audiences (Lee et al. 2017). Moreover, international mainstream media also regarded social media as the source of news during the movements. In the scenes in Tunisia, Egypt and Hong Kong, activists produced their own 'news' on Facebook as 'citizen journalists'. Mainstream news agents, such as *CNN*, *Al Jazeera*, and *Apple Daily*, then navigated social media to collect useful fragments of information for their news reports. Activists, therefore, can reshape the public opinion by approaching to mainstream media.

Through social media use, participants can be mobilised across geographical and political boundaries and across time zones; their actions are decentralised, personalised, and also digitalised; occupation of physical spaces is given more meanings, due to the interpenetration of online and offline activities; and the leadership of the protests is diminished. In both movements, shocking images were recorded and shared widely via social media posts to evoke outrage, disappointment, and grievances among the audiences. By magnifying the violence of police forces, the mediated instant grievance turned the audiences into activists to fight against the oppressive regime. In addition to the emotional factor, some posts launched the call for action by emphasising the political values and the desires of dignity, freedom and democracy. This thesis, however, believes that instead of the complex political statements, the mediated instant grievance is a more straightforward, common and direct emotional factor that resonates and triggers on and offline protest actions on a global scale.

Furthermore, this thesis is aware of the diminishing power of leadership and representation in augmented revolutions. Traditional leaders cannot represent all of the demands of the public and personalised and small-group actions emerged for various purposes. Consequently, the concept of 'soft leader' was developed to comply with the horizontal structure in augmented revolutions. Moreover, when activists fight online and offline simultaneously, the boundary between the actual and virtual dimension was further blurred. The 'villages' that emerged in the Umbrella Movement are an outstanding example of how the relationships in online communities actualise in offline environments and are overlaid on the actual relationships of the protesters. By using social media, contemporary social movements are actually becoming augmented revolutions.

Additionally, comparison of the framing patterns, organisational structures and operational strategies of the Arab Spring and the Umbrella Movement reveals that the close similarity of those factors in both movement, indicating that the Umbrella Movement was an evolved version of the Arab Spring. This thesis therefore contends that when contemporary social movements become augmented revolutions they are contagious, regardless of their political, cultural, and economic differences.

This thesis builds upon the understanding of the potentials of social media and ideally assumes that social media users are interested in political discussions. However, the number of 'likes' and followers on social media cannot guarantee the range and effect of revolutionary messages, as van Dijck cautions (2013). Also, audiences may have no interest, time, or will to participate in a social movement even if they read the messages. In future research, it is important to take into consideration the 'disconnections' of social media use in social movements. How do audiences react to messages on social media when they hold opposite ideas? Moreover, what is the difference between the use of social media in general and a revolutionary situation? My research shows that activists construct their social media posts intentionally in order to summon their friends as well as other audience members to join the protests. However, in daily life, social media is a casual platform for entertainment, chats, and friendship management. These are questions I have not addressed in this thesis and that I will examine in future research projects.

Finally, the thesis notes that despite how significantly social media enhances global communication and facilitates augmented revolution, it is still really digital business platforms, provided and controlled by big corporations. While social media can collaborate with social movements in different economic, political and cultural contexts, such as Islamic (e.g. the MENA region) and capitalist (e.g. US, Hong Kong), it is itself still a product for the global market. The intrinsic value of the profit orientation of social media cannot be neglected in the discussion of augmented revolutions.

First, transnational social media, such as Facebook and Twitter, provides international access in order to boost their advertising profits. However, they need to consider the conditions and obey the policies of local markets. Because of this, some content may be not available for users in certain areas due to the local regulations, or content may be omitted and replaced with something else, if it is recognised as culturally sensitive.

Adjustment of the posts published is a part of the international business strategy of these companies (Deresky 2016). This means that messages relevant to a protest may also be hidden or deleted in keeping with this strategy. Also, social media needs to consider the requests of their business clients to promote or not promote certain movements. The spread of the protests will then be slowed down because message dissemination has been disrupted. This problem was apparent in the process of conducting the case study for this thesis – a large number of valuable archives on Facebook and Twitter that were mentioned in earlier studies are no longer available. The censorship and deletion of posts relevant to the protests may impede future study on augmented revolution. Thus, it is important not to view social media as a privileged space for free expression – it still has its own limitations.

Second, some scholars also consider the argument that social media is not primarily a space for serious political discussions (Lee & Ting 2015; Morozov 2011a). Social media's function as a platform for social networking and maintaining friendships, and for business and business activities such as commercial campaigns and advertising, should take priority over the promotion of social movements. However, the content shared on social media normally does relate to casual topics, such as stories of daily life, jokes, videos, and entertainment. Weibo, the Chinese version of Twitter, can be seen as a notable example of such use, with its users' discussions mainly centred on dramas and gossip about today's superstars. Kim et al. (2013) observe that the more social media users get involved with entertainment related content, the less they are willing to engage with political discussion when they are exposed to it through incidental news. This stance is in line with Postman's (2006) caution regarding "amusing ourselves to death" – he believes that users' constant engagement with entertainment content will distract the public from political issues; when activists share protest relevant messages on social media in order to reach audiences and mobilise them to join social movements, the effects of those messages may be diminished.

Third, in order to improve operations, increase usage and thus enhance competitiveness, developers keep adding more functions to the platforms. These functions may aid activists' efforts, contributing to an 'augmented revolution'. For example, Facebook launched a check-in function in 2010 (Gross & Hanna 2010), which was quickly adopted by activists during the Arab Spring, facilitating the organisation of physical protests actions. Currently, Facebook is also introducing a crisis response function, which allows users involved in a crisis to contact their friends if they are feeling unsafe, or to assure them that they are safe. This function also provides quick access for onlookers to find out more about a particular crisis, to take care of their friends in the danger area, and to support the people there. Meanwhile, the news can be shared widely just by clicking 'Share This Page'. This function is expected to increase the efficiency of the dissemination of information in contemporary social movements. It is the premise of this thesis, that as the social media platforms evolve, their new functions will make still more options available to activists in their campaign operations in protests, and further change the dynamics of

'augmented revolution'.

References

van Aelst, P & Walgrave, S 2004, 'New media, new movement? The role of the internet in shaping the 'anti-globalization' movement'', in W van de Donk, BD Loader, PG Nixon & D Rucht (eds.), *Cyberprotest: New media, citizen and social movements*, Routledge.

Agarwal, N, Lim, M &Wigand RT (ed.) 2014, *Online Collective Action: Dynamics of the Crowd in Social Media*, Springer-Verlag Wien.

Ahy, M 2016, 'Networked Communication and the Arad Spring: Linking broadcast and Social media', *new media & society*, vol.18, no.1, pp. 99-116.

AlSayyad, N 2011, *Cairo: Histories of a City*, MA: Harvard University Press, Cambridge.

AlSayyad, N & Guvenc, M 2015, 'Virtual Uprising: On the Interaction of New Social Media, Traditional Media Coverage and Urban Space during the 'Arab Spring'', *Urban Studies*, August, vol.52, no.11, pp. 2018-2034.

Anduiza, E, Cristancho, C, Sabucedo, JM 2014, 'Mobilization through Online Social Networks: the political protest of the indignados in Spain', *Information, Communication, Society*, July, vol.17, no.6, pp. 750-64.

Arab Centre for Research and Policy Studies 2011, *Revolutions, Reform and Democratic Transition in the Arab Homeland*, Doha institute, Doha.

Asen, R 2000, 'Seeking the "counter" in counterpublics', *Communication Theory*, vol.10, no.4, pp. 424-446.

Ayish, I 2001, 'International communication in the 1900s: implications for the Third World', *International Affairs,* vol.68, no.3, pp. 487–510.

Ayish, M. 2005, 'From "Many voices, one world" to "Many worlds, one voice": Reflections on international communication realities in the age of globalisation', *JAVNOST – THE PUBLIC*, vol.12, no.3, pp. 13–30.

Bandura, A 1986, *Social Foundations of Thought and Actions: A Social Cognitive Theory*, NJ: Prentice-Hall, Englewood Cliffs.

Bandura, A 2002, 'Social cognitive theory of mass communication', in J Bryant & D Zillman (eds), *Media Effects: Advances in Theory and Research*, 2nd edn., NJ: Erlbaum, Hillsdale.

Bauman, Z 1998, *Globalization: the human consequences*, Polity, Cambridge.

Bennett, LW, 2012, 'The personalization of politics: Political identity, social media and changing patterns of participation', *The Annals of the American Academy of Political and Social Science*, vol.644, pp. 20-39.

Bennett, LW & Segerberg, A 2013, *The Logic of Connective Action*, Cambridge University Press, New York.

Benson, M & Rochon T 2004, 'Interpersonal Trust and the Magnitude of Protest: A Micro and Macro Level Approach', *Comparative Political Studies*, vol.37, no.4, pp. 435-57.

Bolter, JD & Grusin, R 2000, *Remediation: understanding new media*, The MIT Press, Cambridge.

Bornman, E & Schoonraad, N 2001, 'Globalisation and international communication: an introduction', in *International communication: only study guide for COM305-C*, E. Bornman, P. Fourie, Z. Lesame and N. Schoonraad (eds), 1–50. Pretoria: Department of Communication, University of South Africa.

Boulding, KE 1959, 'National Images and International Systems', *The Journal of Conflict Resolution*, vol. 3, No. 2, June, pp. 120-31.

boyd, d 2010, 'Social Network Sites as Networked Publics: Affordances, Dynamics, and Implications', In Z, Papacharissi (eds.), *Networked Self: Identity, Community, and Culture on Social Network Sites*, Routledge.

Boykoff, J 2006, *The Suppression of Dissent*, Routledge.

Bruns, A 2008, Blogs, *Wikipedia, Second life and Beyond: from production to produsage*, Peter Lang, New York.

Bruns, A, Highfield, T & Burgess, J 2013, 'The Arab Spring and Social Media Audiences: English and Arabic Twitter Users and Their Networks', *American Behavioral Scientist*, vol.57, no.7, pp. 871-98.

Brym, R, Godbout, M, Hoffbauer, A, Menard, G & Zhang, TH 2014, 'Social Media in the 2011 Egyptian Uprising', *British Journal of Sociology*, vol.65, no.2, pp. 266-92.

Buhler-Muller, N & van der Merwe, C 2011, 'The potential of social media to influence socio-political change on the African Continent', *Africa Institution of South Africa*, Briefing no.46, March, <http://www.ai.org.za/wp-content/uploads/downloads/2011/11/No-46.-The-potential-of-social-media-to-influence-socio-political-change-on-the-African-Continent.pdf>.

Burean, T & Badescu, G 2014, 'Voices of discontent: student protest participation in Romania', *Communist and Post-Communist Studies*, vol. 47, no. 3-4, pp. 385-97.

Calhoun, C 1992, 'Introduction', in C. Calhoun (eds.), *Habermas and the Public Sphere*, MA: The MIT Press, Cambridge.

Carty, V 2015, *Social movements and new technology*, Chapman University.

Castells, M 2009, *Communication Power*, Oxford University Press, Oxford.

Castells, M 2012, *Networks of outrage and hope: Social movements in the Internet age*, MA: Polity Press, Malden.

Chan, DK & Fu, KW 2014, 'Blocks of Facebook special pages in the occupied era', *Ming Pao Daily*, December 2014, p. S07.

Chan, J & Lee, FLF 2007, 'Media and large-scale demonstration: The pro-democracy movement in post-handover Hong Kong', *Asian Journal of Communication*, vol.17, no.2, pp. 215-228.

Chan, J & Lee, FLF 2014, 'Preliminary research on the new organizational forms of occupy movement', *Ming Pao Daily*, p. A29.

Chen, H, Ping, S & Chen, G 2015, 'Far from reach but near at hand: The role of social media for cross-national mobilization', *Computers in Human Behavior*, vol.53, pp. 443-51.

Chiu, CM, Hsu, MH & Wang ET, 2006, 'Understanding Knowledge Sharing in Virtual Communities: An Integration of Social Capital and Social Cognitive Theories', *Decision Support Systems*, vol.42, no.3, pp. 1872-88.

Coleman, J 1988, 'Social Capital in the Creation of Human Capital', *American Journal of Sociology*, vol.94, pp. 95-120.

Dahlgren, P 2005, 'The Internet, Public Sphere, and Political Communication: Dispersion and Deliberation', *Political Communication*, vol.22, no.2, pp. 147-62.

Dean, J 2010, 'Affective networks', *Media Tropes eJournal*, vol.2, no.2, pp. 19-44.

Deleuze, G & Guattari, H 2004, *A thousand plateaus: capitalism and schizophrenia*, Massumi B (trans.), London: Continuum.

Deresky, H 2016, *International Management*, 9th edn, UK: Person.

van Dijck, J 2013, 'Engineering Sociality in a Culture of Connectivity', in *The Culture of Connectivity: A Critical History of Social Media*, Oxford Scholarship online, pp. 1-31.

van de Donk, W, Lodaer BD, Nixion,PG & Rucht (eds.) 2004, *Cyberprotest: New media, citizen and social movements*, Routledge.

Duvenhage, P 2005, 'Habermas, the public sphere and beyond', *Communicatio*, vol.31, no.1, pp. 1-12.

Earl, J & Kimport K 2011, *Digitally Enabled Social Change*, MIT Press, Harvard.

Economy Watch 2015, *Facebook Penetration Rate Data for All Countries*, Economy Watch, 17 March, viewed 18 June 2018, <http://www.economywatch.com/economic-statistics/economic-indicators/Facebook_Penetration_Rate/>.

Flynn, M & Hutcheson, J 2015, 'The 1989 Tiananmen Square Incident', *United Service*, vol.66, no.2, pp. 13-5.

Forde, S 2011, *Challenging the News*, Palgrave McMillan, New York.

Frangonikoloppoulos, CA & Chapsos, I 2012, 'Explaining the Role and the Impact of the Social Media in the Arab Spring', *Global Media Journal*, Mediterranean edition, vol.8, no.1, pp. 10-20.

Fraser, N 1992, 'Rethinking the Public Sphere: A Contribution to the Critique of Actually Existing Democracy', in C. Calhoun (eds.), *Habermas and the Public Sphere*, MA: The MIT Press, Cambridge.

Friedman, TL 2014, 'The square people, part 1', *The New York Times*, 13 May, viewed 23 July 2018, <https://www.nytimes.com/2014/05/14/opinion/friedman-the-square-people-part-1.html?_r=0>.

Fu, KW & Chan, CH 2015, 'Networked collective action in the 2014 Hong Kong Occupy Movement: analysing a Facebook sharing network', *The HKU Scholar Hub*, The University of Hong Kong.

Fuchs, C 2017, *Social Media: a critical introduction*, SAGE.

Galtung, J 1971, 'A structural theory of imperialism', *Journal of Peace Research*, vol.8, pp. 81–117.

Gamson, W, Fireman, B and Rytina, S 1982, *Encounters with Unjust Authority*, Dorsey Press, Homewood.

Gamson, W & Modigliani, A 1989, 'Media discourse and public opinion: A constructionist approach', *American Journal of Sociology*, 95, pp. 1-37.

Gamson, W & Wolfsfeld, G 1993, 'Movements and media as interacting systems', *Annals of the American Academy of Political and Social Science*, vol.528, pp. 114-25.

Gerbaudo, P 2012, *Tweets and the Streets: Social Media and Contemporary Activism*, PlutoPress, London.

Gerlach, LP 2001, 'The structure of social movements: environmental activism and its opponents', in J Arquilla & D Ronfeldt (eds.), *Networks and netwars: the future of terror, crime, and militancy*, Santa Monica: Rand.

Gerlitz, C & Helmond, A 2013, 'The like economy: Social buttons and the data-intensive web', *New Media & Society*, vol.15, no.8, pp. 1349-65.

Giddens, A 1990, *The consequences of modernity*, Cambridge: Polity.

Giddens, A 1991, *Modernity and self-identity: self and society in the modern age*, Cambridge: Polity.

Gitlin, T 1980, *The whole world is watching: Mass media in the making and unmaking of the New Left*, CA: University of California Press, Berkeley.

Givan, R, Roberts, K & Soule, S 2010, 'Introduction', in R. Givan, K. Roberts, & S. Soule (eds.), *The Diffusion of Social Movements: Actors, Mechanisms, and Political Effects*, Cambridge: Cambridge University Press.

Gladwell, M 2010, 'Small Change: Why the revolution will not be tweeted', *The New Yorker*, 4 October, viewed 1 November 2017, <https://www.newyorker.com/magazine/2010/10/04/small-change-malcolm-gladwell>.

Goffman, E 1974, *Frame analysis: An essay on the organization of experience*, New York: Harper & Row.

Gregg, M 2011, *Work's intimacy*, Polity, Cambridge.

Griffiths, J 2014, 'White House calls for 'genuine choice' in Hong Kong elections after petition attracts 200,000 signatures', *South China Morning Post*, 01 October, viewed 28 August 2018, <https://www.scmp.com/news/hong-kong/article/1605310/white-house-calls-genuine-choice-hong-kong-elections-after-petition>.

Gross, D & Hanna, J 2010, 'Facebook introduces check-in feature', *CNN*, 19 August, viewed 17 September 2018, <http://edition.cnn.com/2010/TECH/social.media/08/18/facebook.location/index.html>.

Habermas, J 1987, *Theory of communicative action*, MA: Beacon Press, Boston.

Habermas, J 1989, 'Social Structures of the Public Sphere', in T Burger & F Lawrence (eds.), *The Structural Transformation of the Public Sphere: An Inquiry into a Category of Bourgeois Society*, The MIT Press, Cambridge.

Habermas, J 1992, 'Further reflections on the public sphere and concluding remarks', in C Calhoun (eds.), *Habermas and the public sphere*, MA: MIT Press, Cambridge.

Habermas, J 1999, 'The European nation state and the pressures of globalization', *New Left Review*, vol.235, pp. 46-50.

Habermas, J 2001, *Why Europe needs a constitution*, viewed 21 June 2017, <http://www.newleftreview.net/NLR24501.shtml>.

Habermas, J 2006, 'Political Communication in Media Society: Does Democracy Still Enjoy an Epistemic Dimension? The Impact of Normative Theory on Empirical Research', *Communication Theory: A Journal of the International Communication Association*, vol.16, pp. 411-26.

Halvorsen, S 2015, 'Taking Space: moments of rupture and everyday life in Occupy London', *Antipode*, vol.47, no.2, pp. 401-17.

Hands, J 2011, *@ is for Activism: Dissent, Resistance and Rebellion in a Digital Culture*, Pluto Press.

Haraway, D 2013, *Simians, cyborgs, and women: The reinvention of nature*, Routledge.

Herman, E & Chomsky, N 2002, *Manufacturing consent: the political economy of mass media*, New York: Pantheon Books.

Highfield, T 2016, *Social Media and Everyday Politics*, Polity, Malden.

Howard, P & Hussain, M 2013, *Democracy's Fourth Wave?: Digital Media and the Arab Spring*, Oxford Scholarship Online.

Huat, C 2017, 'Introduction: Inter-referencing East Asian Occupy Movements', *International Journal of Cultural Studies*, vol.20, no.2, pp. 121-26.

Hui, YF 2017, 'The Umbrella Movement: Ethnographic explorations of communal re-spatialization', *International Journal of Cultural Studies*, vol.20, no.2, pp. 146-61.

Jackson, J 2014, *Introducing Language and Intercultural Communication*, Routledge, New York.

Jasper, JM 2010, 'Cultural Approaches in the Sociology of Social Movements', in B Klandermasn & C Roggeband (eds.), *Handbook of Social Movements Across Disciplines*, Springer, New York.

Jenkins, H 2006, *Convergence Culture*, New York University Press, New York.

Joshua: Teenager vs. Superpower 2017, Netflix, viewed 15 June 2018, <https://www.netflix.com/watch/80169348?tctx=0%2C0%2C16f11284-4c73-4979-92f9-c87b3b554443-13323682%2C%2C>.

Jurgenson, N & Ritzer, G 2009, 'Efficiency, Effectiveness and Web 2.0', In S Kleinman (eds.), *The Culture of Efficiency*, Peter Lang: New York.

Jurgenson, N 2011a, 'Why Chomsky is Wrong about Social Media', *Salon*, 23 October, viewed 22 May 2018, <https://www.salon.com/2011/10/23/why_chomsky_is_wrong_about_twitter/>.

Jurgenson, N 2011b, 'Augmented Friendship Illustrated by PEW Date', *The Society Pages*, 16 June, viewed 15 August 2018, <https://thesocietypages.org/cyborgology/2011/06/16/augmented-friendship-illustrated-by-pew-data/>.

Jurgenson, N 2012, 'When Atoms Meet Bits: Social Media, the Moblie Web and Augmented Revolution', *Future Internet*, vol. 4, pp. 83-91.

Karatzogianni, A & Kuntsman, A 2012, *Digital cultures and the politics of emotion: Feelings, affect and technological change*. London: Palgrave Macmillan.

Kim, JW, Kim, Y & Yoo, JJ 2014, 'The public as active agents in social movement: Facebook and Gangjeong Movement', *Computers in Human Behavior*, vol.37, pp. 144-51

Kim, Y, Chen, H & de Zuniga, HG 2013, 'Stumbling upon news on the Internet: Effects of incidental news exposure and relative entertainment use on political engagement', *Computers in Human Behavior*, vol.29, pp. 2607-2614.

Laclau, E 2005, *On populist reason*, Verso, New York.

Lam, L 2014, 'Facebook is Hong Kong's top digital platform in survey commissioned by company', *South China Morning Post*, 22 August, viewed 20 June 2018, <https://www.scmp.com/news/hong-kong/article/1578755/facebook-citys-top-digital-platform-survey-commissioned-company>.

Lee, FLF 2015a, 'Press freedom and political change in Hong Kong', in G, Rawnsley & M, Y, Rawnsley (eds.), *The Routledge Handbook of Chinese Media*, Routledge, London.

Lee, FLF 2015b, 'Media communication and the Umbrella Movement: Introduction to the special issue', *Chinese Journal of Communication*, vol.8, no.4, pp. 333-337.

Lee, FLF & Chan, JM 2008, 'Professionalism, political orientation, and perceived self-censorship: A survey study of Hong Kong journalists', *Issue & Studies*, vol.44, pp. 205-38.

Lee, FLF & Chan, JM 2011, *Media, social mobilization, and mass protest in post-colonial Hong Kong*, Routledge, London.

Lee, FLF & Chan, JM 2015, 'Digital media activities and mode of participation in a protest campaign: The case of Umbrella Movement', *Chinese Journal of Communication*, vol.8, no.4, pp. 393-411.

Lee, FLF & Chan, JM 2018, *Media and Protest Logics in the Digital Era: The Umbrella Movement in Hong Kong*, Oxford University Press.

Lee, FLF, Chen, H & Chan, JM 2017, 'Social media use and university students' participation in a large-scale protest campaign: The case of Hong Kong's Umbrella Movement', *Telematics and Informatics*, vol. 34, pp. 457-69.

Lee, SNP, So, YKC & Leung, L 2015, 'Social media and Umbrella Movement: insurgent public sphere in formation', *Chinese Journal of Communication*, vol.8, no.5, pp. 356-75.

Lee, K 2017, 'Looking back at the candlelight protest of 2008, South Korea: Reflection on its multiple implications and lessons', *International Journal of Cultural Studies*, vol.20, no.2, pp. 193-208.

Lee, YL & Ting, KW 2015, 'Media and information praxis of young activists in the Umbrella Movement', *Chinese Journal of Communication*, vol.8, no.4, pp. 376-92.

Leung, DKK & Lee FLF 2014, 'Cultivating an active online counterpublic: Examining usage and political impact of Internet alternative media', *The International Journal of Press/Politics*, vol.19, no.3, pp. 340-59.

van Leuven, S, Heinrich, A & Deprez, A 2015, 'Foreign reporting and sourcing practices in the network sphere: A quantitative content analysis of the Arab Spring in Belgian news media', *new media & society*, vol.7, no.4, pp. 573-591.

Lim, M 2012, 'Clicks, cabs, and coffee house: Social media and oppositional movements in Egypt, 2004-2011', *Journal of Communication*, vol.62, no.2, pp. 231-48.

Lim, M 2013, 'Framing Bouazizi: 'White lies', hybrid network, and collective/connective action in the 2010-11 Tunisian uprising', *Journalism*, vol.14, no.7, pp. 921-41.

Lim, J 2017, 'Engendering civil resistance: Social media and mob tactics in Malaysia', *International Journal of Cultural Studies*, vol.20, no.2, pp. 209-27.

Lin, Z 2017, 'Contextualized Transmedia Moblization: Media Practice and Mobilizing Structures in the Umbrella Movement', *International Journal of Communication*, vol.11, pp. 48-71.

Ling, RS 2004, *The Mobile Connection: The Cell Phone's Impact on Society*, Morgan Kaufmann, San Francisco.

Loader, B & Mercea, D 2011, 'Networking Democracy?', *Information, Communication & Society*, vol.14, no.6, pp. 757-69.

MacKee, A 2005, *The public sphere: An introduction*, Cambridge University Press.

Madikiza, L & Bornman, E 2007, 'International communication: shifting paradigms, theories and foci of interest', *Communicatio: South African Journal for Communication Theory and Research*, vol.33, no.2, pp. 11-44.

Majerol, V & Perlman, M 2014, 'The Tiananmen Square Protest', *New York Time*, 13 January.

McAdam, D & Paulsen, D 1993, 'Specifying the Relationship between Social Ties and Activism', *American Journal of Sociology*, vol.99, no.3, pp. 640-67.

McAdam, D & Rucht, D 1993, 'The cross-national diffusion of movement ideas', *The Annals of the American Academy of Political and Social Science*, vol. 528, pp. 56-74.

McGarty, C, Thomas, EF, Lala, G, Smith, LGE & Bliuc, AM 2014, 'New technologies, new identities, and the growth of mass opposition in the Arab Spring', *Political Psychol*, vol.35, no. 6, pp. 725-48.

McKee, A 2003, *Textual Analysis*, SAGE, London.

McLuhan, M 1964, 'The Medium is the Message', in *Understanding Media: The Extension of Man*, The MIT Press.

McQuail, D 2005, *McQuail's Mass Communication Theory*, 5th edn., SAGE, London.

Meyerhoff, M 2006, *Introducing Sociolinguistics*, Routledge, Abingdon.

Morozov, E 2009, 'The brave new world of slacktivism', *Foreign Policy*, 19 May, viewed 24 May 2018, <http://foreignpolicy.com/2009/05/19/the-brave-new-world-of-slacktivism/>.

Morozov, E 2011a, *The Net Delusion: how not to liberate the world*, London: Allen Lane.

Morozov, E 2011b, 'Facebook and Twitter are just places revolutionaries go', *The Guardian*, 7 March, viewed 1 November 2017, <http://www.guardian.co.uk/commentisfree/2011/mar/07/facebook-twitter-revolutionaries-cyber-utopians/>.

Nahapiet, J & Ghoshal, S 1998, 'Social Capital, Intellectual Capital, and the Organizational Advantage', *Academy of Management Review*, vol.23, no.2, pp. 242-66.

Negt, O & Kluge, A 1993, *Public sphere and experience: Toward an analysis of the bourgeois and proletarian public sphere*, University of Minnesota Press, Minneapolis.

Nekmat, E 2012, 'Message expression effects in online social communication', *Journal of Broadcasting & Electronic Media*, vol.56, no.2, pp. 203-24.

Nissenbaum, A & Shifman, L 2015, 'Internet memes as contested cultural capital: The case of 4chan's /b/ board', *New Media and Society*, vol.19, no.4, pp. 483-501.

Olorunnisola, AA & Martin, BL 2014, 'Influences of media on social movements: problematizing hyperbolic inferences about impacts', *Telematics and Informatics*, vol.30, no.3, pp. 275-88.

Palczewski, C 2001, 'Cyber-movement: New social movements, and counterpublics', in R Asen & DC Brouwer (eds.), *Counterpublics and the state*, State University of New York Press, Albany.

Pan, Z & Kosicki, GM 1993, 'Framing Analysis: An Approach to News Discourse', *Political Communication*, vol.10, pp. 55-75.

Papacharissi, Z 2010, *A private sphere: Democracy in a digital age*, Polity Press, Cambridge.

Papacharissi, Z 2014, *Affective Publics: Sentiments, Technology and Politics*, Oxford Scholarship Online: Oxford University Press.

Papacharissi, Z & Trevey, M 2018, 'Affective Publics and Windows of Opportunity: Social media and the potential for social change', in Meikle, G (eds.), *The Routledge Companion to Media and Activism*, Routledge, Oxon.

Pateman, C 1989, *The disorder of women: Democracy, feminism, and political theory*, Polity Press, Cambridge.

Pickerill, J & Krinsky, J 2012, 'Why does occupy matter?', *Social Movement Studies*, vol.11, no.3, pp. 279-87.

Poell, T & Darmoni, K 2012, 'Twitter as a Multilanguage space: The articulation of the Tunisian revolution through #sidibouzid', *NECSUS: European Journal of Media Studies*, vol.1, no.1, pp. 14-34.

Potts, J 2015, *The New Time and Space*, Palgrave Macmillan, UK.

Postman, N 2006, *Amusing Ourselves to Death: Public discourse in the age of show business*, Penguin Books, New York.

Rane, H & Salem, S 2012, 'Social media, social movements and the diffusion of ideas in the Arab uprisings', *The Journal of International Communication*, 18:1, pp. 97-111.

Rantanen, T 2005, *The media and globalization*, Sage, London.

Rheingold, H 2002, *Smart Mobs*, New York: Basic Books,

Ritzer, G 2015, 'The "New" World of Prosumption: Evolution, "Return of the Same", or Revolution?', *Sociological Forum*, vol.30, no.1, March, pp. 1-17.

Ritzer, G & Jurgenson, N 2010, 'Production, Consumption, Prosumption: The nature of capitalism in the age of the digital "prosumer"', *Journal of Consumer Culture*, vol.10, no.1, pp. 13-36.

Ritzer, G, Dean, P & Jurgenson N 2012, 'The Coming of Age of the Prosumer', *American Behavioral Scientist*, vol.56, no.4, pp. 379-98.

Robertson, R 1992, *Globalization: social theory and global culture*, London: Sage.

Rogers, E 2003, *Diffusion of Innovations* (5th ed.), New York: Free Press.

Roggeband, C& Klandermans, B 2010, 'Introduction', in B Klandermasn & C Roggeband (eds.), *Handbook of Social Movements Across Disciplines*, Springer, New York.

Salem, F. & Mourtada, R. (2011) 'Facebook usage: Factors and analysis', *Arab Social Media Report (ASMR)*, vol.1, no.1, pp. 1-18.

Schroeder, R, Everton, E & Shepherd, R 2014, 'The Strength of Tweet Ties', in N, Agrwal, M, Lim & R Wigand (eds.), *Online Collective Action: Dynamics of the Crowd in Social Media*, Springer, Wien.

Seargeant, P & Tagg, C 2013, 'Introduction: The language of social media', in P, Seargeant & C, Tagg (ed.), *the language of social media: identity and community on the internet*, Palgrave Macmillan, UK.

Shirky, C 2008, *Here comes everybody*, London: Penguin.

Shirky, C 2011, 'The political power of social media: technology, the public sphere, and political change', *Foreign Affairs*, vol.90, no.1, January, pp. 28-41.

Skinner, J 2011, 'Social Media and Revolution: The Arab Spring and the Occupy Movement as Seen through Three Information Studies Paradigms', *Sprouts: Working Paper on Information Systems*, vol.11, no.169, <http://sprouts.aisnet.org/11-169>.

Smith, J & Fetner, T 2010, 'Structural Approaches in the Sociology of Social Movements', in B Klandermasn & C Roggeband (eds.), *Handbook of Social Movements Across Disciplines*, Springer, New York.

Snow, DA, Rochford, EB, Worden, SK & Benford, RD 1986, 'Frame alignment processes: Micromobilization and movement participation', *American Sociological Review*, vol.51, no.4, pp. 464-481.

So, CYK, 2014, 'The generation divide of the media audience', *Ming Pao Daily*, 16 October, p. D5.

Soule, S 2004, 'Diffusion process within and across social movements', in D, Snow, S, Soule & H, Kriesi (eds.), *The Blackwell Companion to Social Movements*, Blackwell, Malden.

Spilerman, S 1976, "Structural characteristics of cities and the severity of radical disorders", *American Sociological Review*, vol. 41, No. 5, pp. 771-93.

Squires, C 2002, 'Rethinking the black public sphere: An alternative vocabulary for multiple public spheres', *Communication Theory*, vol.12, no.4, pp. 446-68.

van Stekelenburg, J & Klandermans, B 2010, 'Individals in Movements: A Social Psychology of Contention', in B Klandermasn & C Roggeband (eds.), *Handbook of Social Movements Across Disciplines*, Springer, New York.

Suh, CS, Vasi, IB & Chang PY 2017, 'How social media matter: Repression and the diffusion of the Occupy Wall Street movement', *Social Science Research*, vol.65, pp. 282-93.

Tang, G 2015, 'Mobilization by images: TV screen and mediated instant grievances in the Umbrella Movement', *Chinese Journal of Communication*, vol.8, no.4, pp. 338-55.

Tarrow, S 1998, *Power in Movement*, Cambridge University Press, Cambridge.

Tehranian, M 1999, *Global communications and world politics: domination, development, and discourse*, Lynne Riener, Boulder.

Thussu, DK 2000, *International communication: continuity and change*. London: Arnold.

Toffler, A 1980, *The third wave*, New York, William Morrow.

Tsui, L 2015, 'The coming colonization of Hong Kong cyberspace: government responses to the use of new technologies by the umbrella movement', *Chinese Journal of Communication*, vol.8, no.4. p. 1-9.

Tufekci, Z 2013, '"Not this one": social movements, the attention economy, and microcelebrity networked activism', *American Behavioral Scientist*, vol.57, no.7, pp. 848-70.

Wang, C 2017a, '"The future that belongs to us': Affective politics, neoliberalism, and the Sunflower Movement', *International Journal of Cultural Studies*, vol.20, no.2, pp. 177-92.

Wang, KJY 2017b, 'Mobilizing resources to the square: Hong Kong's Anti-Moral and National Education movement as precursor to the Umbrella Movement', *International Journal of Cultural Studies*, vol.20, no.2, pp. 127-145.

Wang, R, Kin, J, Xiao, A & Jung, JY 2017, 'Networked narratives on Humans of New York: A content analysis of social media engagement on Facebook', *Computer in Human Behavior*, vol.66, pp. 149-53.

Warner, M 2002, *Publics and Counterpublics*, MA: MIT Press, Cambridge.

Warren, AM, Sulaiman, A, Jaafar, NI, 2015, 'Understanding civic engagement behavior on Facebokk from a social capital theory perspective', *Behaviour & Information Technology*, vol.32, no.2, pp. 163-75.

Waters, M 1995, *Globalization*, Routledge, London.

Wesch, M 2008, 'Context collapse', *Digital Ethnography @ Kansas State University*, viewed 25 March 2018, <http://mediatedcultures.net/projects/youtube/context-collapse>.

Whitaker, B 2003, 'Battle Station', *The Guardian*, 7 February, viewed 15 August 2018,<https://www.theguardian.com/media/2003/feb/07/iraqandthemedia.afghanistan>.

Wijetunge, D 2014, 'The Digital Divide Objectified in the Design: Use of the Mobile Telephone by Underprivileged Youth in Sri Lanka', *Journal of Computer-Mediated Communication*, vol.19, no.3, pp. 712-26.

Wilson, C & Dunn, A 2011, 'Digital Media in the Egyptian Revolution: Descriptive Analyses from the Tahrir Data Set', *International Journal of Communication*, vol.5, pp. 1248-1272.

Wong, JCF 2015, *I am not a hero*, Crystal Window Book, Hong Kong.

Wong, YC, Fung, JYC, Law, CK, Lam, JCY & Lee, VWP 2009, 'Tackling the Digital Divide', *British Journal of Social Work*, vol.39, pp. 754-67.

Yates, L 2015, 'Rethinking prefiguration: Alternatives, micropolitics and goals in social movements', *Social Movement Studies*, vol.14, no.1, pp. 1-21.

Yuen, S 2015, 'Hong Kong After the Umbrella Movement: An uncertain future for "One Country Two Systems"', *China Perspectives*, vol.1, no.101, pp. 49-53.

van Zoonen, L 2005, *Entertaining the citizen: When politics and popular culture converge*, MD: Rowman & Littlefield, Lanham.

Zuckermen, E 2011, 'The first twitter revolution?', *Foreign Policy*, 15 January, viewed 15 June 2018, <https://foreignpolicy.com/2011/01/15/the-first-twitter-revolution-2/>.

Milton Keynes UK
Ingram Content Group UK Ltd.
UKHW010657220923
429186UK00001B/121